THE NEW SLOW COOKER COOKBOOK

More Than 200 Modern,
Healthy—and Easy—Recipes
for the Classic Cooker

Aadamsmedia
Avon, Massachusetts

Published by
Adams Media, a division of F+W Media, Inc.
57 Littlefield Street, Avon, MA 02322, U.S.A.
www.adamsmedia.com

Contains material adapted from *The Everything® Healthy Slow Cooker Cookbook* by Rachel Rappaport with B.E. Horton, MS, RD, copyright © 2010 by F+W Media, Inc., ISBN 10: 1-4405-0231-5, ISBN 13: 978-1-4405-0231-6.

ISBN 10: 1-4405-9411-2
ISBN 13: 978-1-4405-9411-3
eISBN 10: 1-4405-9412-0
eISBN 13: 978-1-4405-9412-0

Printed in the United States of America.

10 9 8 7 6 5 4 3 2

Always follow safety and commonsense cooking protocol while using kitchen utensils, operating ovens and stoves, and handling uncooked food. If children are assisting in the preparation of any recipe, they should always be supervised by an adult.

Many of the designations used by manufacturers and sellers to distinguish their products are claimed as trademarks. Where those designations appear in this book and F+W Media, Inc. was aware of a trademark claim, the designations have been printed with initial capital letters.

Cover design by Erin Alexander.
Cover images © iStockphoto.com/Nicoolay.
Interior images © iStockphoto.com.

This book is available at quantity discounts for bulk purchases.
For information, please call 1-800-289-0963.

Contents

Introduction

If you thought slow cookers were a thing of the past, think again! Today, this durable cookware is making a comeback and, with *The New Slow Cooker Cookbook*, you'll find yourself impressing your guests with healthy, delicious meals in no time.

Throughout the book, you'll find more than 200 modern, mouth-watering dishes that can be assembled in the morning and eaten immediately when you get home from work or a day out with friends. From breakfast to entrées to sweets and desserts, you'll learn how to prepare your favorite recipes in a new, more wholesome way. And, whether you're a pro or have never used the classic cooker, you'll soon find yourself whipping up dishes like Pear Oatmeal, Green Curry Wings, and Pork Tenderloin with Fennel with confidence and ease.

You may also be wondering how you should go about choosing a slow cooker in the first place, or which ingredients are slow-cooker friendly. Can you use your family's hand-me-down or should you buy something new? Is cooking with one really as simple as tossing lean meats, fresh vegetables, and spices together? And, once you've cooked with your slow cooker, how do you get it clean? All these questions and more will be answered in Chapter 1, which tells you everything you need to know about making easy, flavorful, and nutritious meals in a slow cooker.

So, grab that slow cooker and get ready to make the old new again!

COOKING HEALTHY MEALS IN THE SLOW COOKER

Coming home to a delicious, home-cooked meal is the perfect end to a hard day of work or a busy day running errands. Luckily, it is easy to do just that when you use your slow cooker. This chapter will guide you through the process of becoming adept at making flavorful, healthful meals in your slow cooker. Learn about the benefits of slow cooking, the various types of slow cookers, slow cooker–friendly ingredients, and even how to convert some of your favorite recipes into slow cooker recipes.

The Benefits of Slow Cooking

The benefits of slow cooking are numerous. Slow cookers can be used to make main dishes, one-pot meals, side dishes, even desserts. Most recipes call for a few minutes of prep time and zero hands-on time during the actual cooking. For a small amount of effort in the morning, you can come home to a hot meal after a full day. The recipes with shorter cooking times are perfect for those instances when time is limited, such as when you're running errands, throwing a party, or trying to fit in a meal during the holidays.

The long cooking times associated with most slow cooker recipes mean that cheaper, leaner

cuts of meat come out just as tender as a $30 well-marbled steak. You can turn affordable root vegetables into mouth-watering soups, stews, and side dishes with minimal effort. You can also make pantry staples such as homemade stocks, barbecue sauce, pasta sauces, and even granola for mere pennies in the slow cooker.

While slow cookers are closely associated with wintertime stews, soups, and roasts, they are wonderful to use year-round. Since they do not heat the house the way oven or stovetop cooking does, slow cookers are perfect for warm weather, too. In-season fruits and vegetables at the peak of their flavor and nutritional value make excellent additions to slow cooker dishes.

Although cooking on the grill or stovetop may be faster, it requires a lot more hands-on time and attention. A piece of meat left cooking in a skillet unattended will burn. Soups or sauces left unstirred will thicken, burn, and stick to the pot. These are not issues that occur with a slow cooker. Since a slow cooker uses low, indirect heat, there is no reason to stir or watch the food as it cooks. In fact, there is virtually no risk of burning food in the slow cooker, which makes it a perfect fit for the busy or distracted cook.

Healthy Choices
It is quite easy to make healthy food in the slow cooker. Very little oil or fat is needed because keeping ingredients from sticking to

the cooker is not an issue. Since liquids do not evaporate in the slow cooker, very lean meats will not dry out or overcook the way they might on the stovetop or grill, leaving them amazingly tender. Additionally, using lean meats ensures that your chili, soup, or roast won't be unappetizingly greasy.

Whole grains such as rolled oats, wheat berries, barley, rice, and corn are all well suited to use in the slow cooker. A variety of dishes incorporate nuts and seeds, a wonderful way to introduce healthy fats and fiber into your diet. High-fiber fruits, vegetables, and legumes are at the center of most slow cooker meals.

Types and Sizes of Slow Cookers

Slow cookers have come a long way from their avocado-green, one-size-fits-all days. Now they're available in several sizes and with many modern features. The small 1½- or 2-quart slow cooker is perfect for smaller families and couples. The 4-quart cooker, the most popular size, is capable of making meals that serve four to six people. The largest models are 6–7 quarts and can feed a crowd of eight or more. Hamilton Beach manufactures a three-in-one slow cooker that comes with a set of 2-, 4-, and 6-quart ceramic inserts that can be used one at a time in the same base, eliminating the need to own multiple slow cookers.

Settling on Settings

Look for slow cookers that have at least a low and high setting. This is standard for the mid- to large-size models, but many 2-quart models only have an on/off option. Temperature control is essential if you make full meals in a small slow cooker. Slow cookers equipped solely with an on/off switch are suitable only for keeping fondues, dips, or beverages warm.

Is it time for a new slow cooker?

You can check that your slow cooker is cooking food to the proper temperature by conducting a simple test. Fill the slow cooker two-thirds of the way with water. Cover and cook on low for 8 hours. The temperature of the water at the end of the cooking time should be 185°F. If it is not, replace your slow cooker.

Lifestyle Choices

It is important to choose a slow cooker with features that fit your lifestyle. Many slow cookers have a warm setting that will keep your food warm at approximately 160°F. This is a manual setting on all slow cookers, but on digital models it will also automatically turn on after the programmed cooking time has finished. The automatic switch to warm is especially helpful for people who are not sure exactly when they will be home for dinner. If you enjoy cooking large cuts of meat, look for a model that comes with a probe thermometer that takes an exact temperature of the food inside. Once the meat reaches the desired temperature, the slow cooker will switch to warm to avoid overcooking. If you plan to take your slow cooker to parties or potlucks, there are several models that have secure latches to hold the lid on while in transit. Some models made for travel come with built-in serving spoon holders and rests. There are also models that have an insulated case for the stoneware insert. If cutting down on the number of dirty dishes is important, look for a slow cooker that has an insert that can be placed on top of the stove. Those inserts can brown meats and vegetables and can be put back in the base to finish cooking.

What is the difference between a slow cooker and a Crock-Pot?

Crock-Pots and slow cookers are the same thing. Although the term Crock-Pot is frequently used generically, it is actually a registered trademark for a specific brand of slow cooker. Different brands of cookers may vary in appearance and features, but all function essentially the same way.

Shape Matters

For most recipes, you can use either an oval or a round slow cooker. However, for roasts, meatloaf, or lasagna, or for slow-cooking large pieces of fish, an oval cooker is preferable because it allows the food to lie flat. You can use whatever slow cooker you have on hand, though, since all the recipes in this book can be made using either shape.

The Perfect Ingredients

Nearly any food works well in the slow cooker, but certain ingredients are especially well suited to slow cooking.

Canned Goods

Evaporated milk is shelf-stable canned milk, which is made by removing 60 percent of the water from regular milk. When mixed with an equal amount of water, evaporated milk becomes the equivalent of fresh milk. Rehydration is often unnecessary in slow cooking. Using the evaporated milk straight from the can is a great way to add a creamy dairy flavor. Unlike fresh milk, evaporated milk is safe to use in recipes with long cooking times without fear of curdling.

Canned beans are precooked and recipe-ready, unlike dried beans, which still need to be soaked and fully cooked before being added to the slow cooker. Beans are a wonderful source of protein and fiber and are virtually fat free. Be sure to drain and rinse canned beans prior to use. You can substitute cooked, rehydrated dried beans equally for canned.

Canned tomatoes are better-tasting than out-of-season fresh tomatoes. Unless otherwise noted, add the juice to the slow cooker along with the tomatoes. It can add much-needed moisture to a dish without having to add water or broth.

Produce

Onions are essential to many slow-cooking recipes. Because of their high moisture content, onions give off a lot of liquid as they cook. Instead of adding water or broth to a recipe, which can dilute the flavor of the dish, try onions to provide both moisture and flavor. Onions are especially useful when cooking large cuts of meat or other dishes where you want a drier final product.

Root vegetables such as carrots, parsnips, beets, celeriac, rutabagas, turnips, and potatoes are exceptionally suited to the slow cooker because they retain their shape and texture even after being cooked for hours. Peel carrots, beets, rutabagas, turnips, and parsnips before using them. Potatoes can be used peeled or unpeeled.

Corn, broccoli, cabbage, snow peas, green beans, apples, pears, mangoes, figs, cranberries, strawberries, raspberries, blackberries, blueberries, and tomatoes are all suitable for slow cooking and are high in dietary fiber, which is essential to digestive tract health.

Boost Your Meal's Nutrition

Vegetables can lose valuable nutrients during long cooking times. Blanching the vegetables by cooking them briefly in boiling water helps them retain vitamins. Sautéing vegetables prior to adding them to the slow cooker also optimizes nutrient retention.

Stock Tips

Stock—whether beef, chicken, turkey, vegetable, or seafood—can be used instead of water in almost any dish made in the slow cooker. Recipes made with stock are more flavorful than those made with water. For best results, use salt-free, fat-free stock.

Cooking with Meat

Lean cuts of meat are perfect for the slow cooker. The long cooking time tenderizes the meat, leaving it fork tender. Additionally, using lean meat in dishes such as chili is necessary because there is no way to skim off the fat after cooking. When cooking with beef, look for the least-marbled cuts; choose lean cuts such as tri-tip, top or bottom round roast, top sirloin, or flat half-brisket, all of which meet the governmental standards for very lean or lean meats. When shopping for pork, look for pork tenderloin, boneless pork loin chop, and boneless pork top loin, all of which contain less than 5 percent fat per serving. Boneless, skinless chicken breasts and thighs are also great sources of lean protein. Most grocery stores carry 94 percent lean ground chicken, turkey, pork, and beef.

Adapting Standard Recipes

Although there are many recipes for the slow cooker, you can never have too many. Converting regular recipes so that they can be made in the slow cooker can be a rewarding experience. Long simmering, braising, stewing, and slow-roasting recipes, most of which require more than 1 hour of cooking time on the stovetop or in the oven, can be converted into slow cooker recipes. The slow cooker versions will require far less hands-on time and will have similar (or identical) final products. The most successful converted recipes require the majority of the work in the preparation. While some ingredients can be added to the slow cooker toward the end of the cooking time, recipes that are labor-intensive or that require many steps may not be well suited to this method.

Understanding how a slow cooker works will help you successfully adapt your recipes. Slow cookers have a ceramic insert that is surrounded by a heating element; this configuration keeps the temperature inside constant. The lid traps the heat and moisture so there is little evaporation. Temperatures can vary depending on the age and model of the slow cooker, but as a general rule, the low setting is 170°F and the high is 200°F. Food cooked on low takes roughly twice as long as food cooked on high.

Soups and Stews

The easiest type of recipe to convert is a soup or stew. Follow the preparation of the original recipe, but leave out ingredients such as cooked poultry, rice, pasta, or quinoa and stop short of simmering. Add any browned meats, vegetables, and broth to the slow cooker and cook on low for 8 hours. Add the cooked poultry, rice, pasta, or quinoa during the last 30 minutes of cooking to avoid overcooking it. The lack of evaporation and constant heat ensure that stews will never dry out and soups will cook without boiling over or evaporating.

Liquid Assets

Although a lack of evaporation is not an issue when it comes to cooking soups, the amount of liquid in most other types of recipes needs to be reduced when making adjustments for the slow cooker. Regular recipes assume some liquid will evaporate during the cooking time. Additionally, some ingredients, such as onions, meats, peppers, and tomatoes, give off a lot of liquid as they slow-cook. It is better to err on the side of caution and at least halve the amount of liquid in a traditional recipe. If after slow cooking too much liquid is left, you can still save the dish. For a small amount of excess liquid, remove the lid of the slow cooker and cook on high for 30 minutes to allow for some evaporation. If a lot of liquid remains, drain it off and reduce it in a pot on the stove.

Cooking Seafood

Seafood can be cooked in the slow cooker, but use caution because seafood can easily over-cook. Most seafood should be added during the last 15 to 30 minutes of cooking. The only exceptions are oily fish such as salmon, which can be cooked up to 2 hours on low with no ill effect. In fact, the fish will be amazingly tender and moist due to the lack of evaporation.

Meat

Meat does not brown in the slow cooker. If you want browning for flavor or aesthetic reasons, you need to brown the meat before adding it to the slow cooker. Quickly searing meat in a dry skillet or sautéing it can accomplish this. For stews that need a thicker broth, toss the meat in flour prior to sautéing to help with both browning and thickening. Slow cooking is perfect for recipes that call for cheaper, leaner cuts of meat that need a long cooking time to become tender. For best results, surround the meat with carrots, celery, fennel, or raw or caramelized onions, which will provide the necessary moisture and flavor.

If the original recipe calls for a high-fat cut of meat, substitute a leaner cut. High-fat meats are not well suited to the slow cooker because they become greasy and tough. For example, instead of using bone-in pork shoulder, use pork tenderloin.

Boneless cuts of chicken, turkey, and duck cook relatively quickly in the slow cooker; do not cook them for longer than 4 hours on low or 2 hours on high. Boneless poultry works best in the slow cooker when it is paired with wet ingredients such as sauces, tomatoes, or soft fruit. This ensures that the lean meat will not dry out during the cooking time.

Dairy Dos and Don'ts

Dairy products such as sour cream, cream cheese, and milk do not hold up well over long cooking times. To avoid curdling, add them during the last half hour of cooking. If you are making a hot dip, do not heat it for more than an hour unless otherwise instructed. If milk is a major ingredient, for example, in a creamy sauce or soup, substitute an equal amount of evaporated milk. Evaporated milk can be used directly from the can, and since it has been heat-processed, it can withstand long cooking times. Because of the relatively short, low-heat cooking time of the last half hour, reduced-fat sour cream, cream cheese, and milk can be used with great success in the slow cooker despite having a tendency to separate when cooked using traditional methods.

Start on Low

Most savory recipes can be cooked on low for 8 hours to no ill effect. When in doubt, cook a recipe on low. It is virtually impossible to overcook food in the slow cooker. However, if the food is not fully cooked at the end of the cooking time, turning the temperature to high will help speed up the cooking process. Keep in mind that cooking for 1 hour on high is equal to 2 hours on low, so be sure to keep an eye on the time and occasionally check your recipe to see if it has cooked all the way through.

Keep It Spicy

Experimenting with different flavor combinations is part of the fun of slow cooking. It is also a wonderful way to add flavor to a dish without adding fat. You can use herbs and spices in the same amounts as you would with other cooking methods. Using fresh spices is essential. As spices age, they lose their potency. Taste what you are making before you serve it. If the finished dish is too bland, stir in additional spices prior to serving. Adding soft vegetables such as fresh or frozen peas and corn during the last 30 to 60 minutes of cooking is another way to perk up the flavor of a dish.

Pantry Essentials

Keeping a well-stocked pantry is essential. Having basic yet versatile ingredients on hand makes it easy to prepare a home-cooked meal on the spur of the moment.

Cabinet Staples

Recipes from a wide range of cuisines incorporate canned goods such as fat-free evaporated milk, fat-free sweetened condensed milk, black beans, kidney beans, cannellini beans, black olives, crushed tomatoes, whole tomatoes, tomato paste, and diced tomatoes. Look for low-sodium versions to help reduce your salt intake. Keeping these canned goods on hand will enable you to throw together a delicious, nutritious meal at the last minute.

Stock sold in cartons is generally better tasting than canned and does not need to be refrigerated until opened. Although it is not as tasty as homemade stock, it is helpful to have a few cartons on hand. Buy fat-free, salt-free stock.

Small pastas like orzo, acini di pepe, pastina, alfabeto, and ditalini are perfect for adding to soups. Look for whole-wheat versions for added fiber.

All-purpose flour, cornmeal, baking powder, canola oil, olive oil, wheat berries, barley, and rolled oats are all great in the slow cooker and they have long shelf lives. Additionally, dried fruits and sun-dried tomatoes can be kept on hand to toss in a dish for extra flavor and fiber.

International Cooking Made Easy

Cans of chipotle peppers in adobo, chopped green chiles, hot sauces, and tomatoes with green chiles are all shelf stable. Keep them on hand for making chili, tortilla soup, tamale pie, and other spicy Mexican dishes.

Fish sauce, dark and light soy sauce, chili-garlic sauce, rice vinegar, rice noodles, sesame oil, and Chinese cooking wine can be found in most well-stocked grocery stores. These ingredients are indispensable in Asian recipes.

Spice It Up

A well-stocked spice cabinet is essential for making tasty slow cooker dishes. Ground chipotle, paprika, black pepper, chili powder, ground jalapeño, hot Mexican chili powder, and cayenne pepper can add heat and a depth of flavor to almost any dish. Dried herbs such as oregano, celery flakes, chervil, thyme, rosemary, dill weed, and parsley add a lot of flavor and have a long shelf life. Aromatic spices including cloves, cumin, allspice, nutmeg, cinnamon, and cocoa can be used in savory or sweet dishes. Additional spices that are used less frequently but are still helpful to have around include fennel seed, fenugreek, sumac, mustard seeds, garlic powder, onion powder, diced onion, dill seed, caraway seed, and Chesapeake Bay seasoning.

Storing Other Ingredients

While not technically pantry ingredients, ground meats, chicken breasts and thighs, pork chops, cooked chicken or turkey, and salmon freeze well and can be defrosted in the refrigerator overnight. Minced fresh herbs can be frozen and used directly from the freezer in any recipe that calls for fresh herbs.

Properly stored in cool, dark places, potatoes, apples, parsnips, rutabagas, and winter squash can last an entire season. Stock up and have them on hand at all times for easy yet flavorful meals.

Slow-Cooking Tips

The first time you use a slow cooker, you'll find it helpful to be home to check on the dish to see how it is cooking. Some slow cookers may run hotter or cooler than others, and it is important to know whether the cooking time needs to be adjusted. Additionally, you don't want to come home to a cold, raw meal because the slow cooker did not turn on or work properly.

Slow cookers work best when they are at least one-half to two-thirds full. Less food will cook more quickly and less evenly. For best results, choose a slow cooker or insert that is the proper size for the recipe.

Pay attention to layering instructions. Place slower-cooking ingredients such as root vegetables near the bottom of the slow cooker unless otherwise noted.

Remove any visible fat from meat before adding it to the slow cooker. Also be sure to drain off any rendered fat before putting browned meat in the slow cooker.

Safety First

Heating an empty ceramic insert may cause it to crack. Be sure the insert is at room temperature when placed in the slow cooker base. Sudden changes in temperature can also cause cracks in the ceramic insert, such as putting a hot insert into cool water in the sink.

Defrost all frozen meats and vegetables in the refrigerator before placing them in the slow cooker. The food in the slow cooker must reach the safe temperature of 140°F as soon as possible. Using frozen meat may lower the temperature of the dish into the danger zone for an extended period. Small frozen vegetables such as peas and corn will not lower the temperature enough to be dangerous, but add them toward the end of the cooking time for best texture and flavor.

To keep the temperature constant in the slow cooker, avoid removing the lid during the cooking time. Removing the lid can reduce the temperature in the cooker, adding to the overall cooking time. Additionally, do not repeatedly add new items to the slow cooker during the cooking process. It can cause the internal temperature to dip below what is considered safe. If additional ingredients need to be added, they should be added all at once toward the end of the cooking time.

Food Safety Tips

Refrigerate leftovers within 2 hours of finishing cooking. It is not safe to keep the food warm in the slow cooker indefinitely, so be sure to only leave it on the warm setting for a maximum of 2 hours. Serving utensils can introduce bacteria to the food that will not be killed off by the low temperatures of the warm setting. Reheat leftovers in the oven, on the stovetop, or in the microwave.

The outside of some slow cookers can become quite hot. Do not place flammable items or items that may melt near the slow cooker while it is in use. All modern slow cookers have short cords to reduce the risk of tipping over, but it is still important to keep them away from small children and pets. Contents in the slow cooker can be near boiling temperatures and the hot exteriors can cause burns or skin irritation.

BREAKFASTS AND BRUNCHES

Wheat Berry Breakfast

1. Add the wheat berries, water, and cranberries to a 2- or 4-quart slow cooker. Stir. Cook on low for 8–10 hours.

2. Stir before serving to distribute the cranberries evenly.

1 cup wheat berries

2½ cups water

¼ cup sweetened dried cranberries

Per Serving

Calories	Fat	Sodium	Carbohydrates	Fiber	Protein
120	3.5g	0mg	27g	4g	3g

Southern-Style Grits

Add the grits, Chicken Stock, pepper, and salt to a 4-quart slow cooker. Stir. Cook on low for 8 hours. Top with cheese before serving.

1½ cups stone-ground grits

4¼ cups Chicken Stock (Chapter 4) or water

½ teaspoon freshly ground black pepper

¼ teaspoon salt

¼ cup shredded reduced-fat sharp Cheddar

Per Serving

Calories	Fat	Sodium	Carbohydrates	Fiber	Protein
80	0.5g	50mg	16g	0g	2g

Southern-Style Grits

Hearty Multigrain Cereal

1. Add the wheat berries, rice, oats, and water to a 2- or 4-quart slow cooker. Stir. Cook on low for 8–10 hours.

2. Stir before serving.

¼ cup wheat berries

¼ cup long-grain rice

1 cup rolled or Irish-style oats

3½ cups water

Per Serving

Calories	Fat	Sodium	Carbohydrates	Fiber	Protein
150	2.5g	0mg	30g	4g	5g

Hash Browns

1. Heat oil in a nonstick skillet. Add bacon, onions, and potatoes. Sauté until just browned. The potatoes should not be fully cooked.

2. Add mixture to a 2- or 4-quart slow cooker. Cook on low for 3–4 hours or on high for 1½ hours.

1 teaspoon canola oil

2 strips turkey bacon, diced

1 large onion, thinly sliced

1½ pounds red skin potatoes, thinly sliced

Per Serving

Calories	Fat	Sodium	Carbohydrates	Fiber	Protein
170	3g	95mg	31g	3g	5g

Pear Oatmeal

Place all ingredients in a 4-quart slow cooker. Cook on low overnight (8–9 hours). Stir and serve.

2 Bosc pears, cored and sliced thinly

2¼ cups pear cider or water

1½ cups old-fashioned rolled oats

1 tablespoon dark brown sugar

½ teaspoon cinnamon

Per Serving

Calories	Fat	Sodium	Carbohydrates	Fiber	Protein
220	2.5g	0mg	43g	7g	6g

French Toast Casserole

1. Spray a 4-quart slow cooker with nonstick spray. Layer the bread in the slow cooker.
2. In a small bowl, whisk the eggs, vanilla, evaporated milk, brown sugar, cinnamon, and nutmeg. Pour over the bread.
3. Cover and cook on low for 6–8 hours. Remove the lid and cook uncovered for 30 minutes or until the liquid has evaporated.

12 slices whole-grain raisin bread

6 eggs

1 teaspoon vanilla

2 cups fat-free evaporated milk

2 tablespoons dark brown sugar

1 teaspoon cinnamon

¼ teaspoon nutmeg

Per Serving

Calories	Fat	Sodium	Carbohydrates	Fiber	Protein
230	6g	280mg	32g	2g	13g

Spinach Mushroom Quiche

Spinach Mushroom Quiche

SERVES 6

1. Spray a round 4-quart slow cooker with nonstick cooking spray. In a small bowl, whisk the cayenne, eggs, cheese, spinach, mushrooms, evaporated milk, and green onions.

2. Add the bread cubes in one layer on the bottom of the slow cooker. Pour the egg mixture over the top and cover. Cook on high for 2–3 hours or until the edges begin to pull away from the sides of the insert. Slice, and lift out each slice individually.

1 teaspoon cayenne

4 eggs

½ cup shredded reduced-fat sharp Cheddar

6 ounces baby spinach

4 ounces chopped cremini mushrooms

1½ cups fat-free evaporated milk

¼ cup diced green onion

2 slices sandwich bread, cubed

Per Serving

Calories	Fat	Sodium	Carbohydrates	Fiber	Protein
160	6g	220mg	16g	2g	13g

Breakfast Quinoa with Fruit

SERVES 4

Place all ingredients in a 4-quart slow cooker. Stir. Cook on high for 2–3 hours or until the quinoa is fully cooked.

1 cup quinoa

2 cups water

½ cup dried mixed berries

1 pear, thinly sliced

1 teaspoon dark brown sugar

½ teaspoon ground ginger

¼ teaspoon cinnamon

⅛ teaspoon ground cloves

⅛ teaspoon nutmeg

Per Serving

Calories	Fat	Sodium	Carbohydrates	Fiber	Protein
250	3g	10mg	51g	5g	6g

Pear, Apple, and Cranberry Pancake Topping

Place all ingredients in a 2-quart slow cooker. Stir. Cook on low for 2 hours.

3 tart apples, thinly sliced

3 Bosc pears, thinly sliced

¾ cup fresh cranberries

1 tablespoon brown sugar

½ teaspoon ground ginger

½ teaspoon cinnamon

¼ teaspoon nutmeg

¼ teaspoon mace

Per Serving

Calories	Fat	Sodium	Carbohydrates	Fiber	Protein
70	0g	0mg	19g	4g	0g

Cheese "Soufflé"

1. Mix the cheeses and set aside. Tear the bread into large pieces and set aside. Spray a 4-quart slow cooker with non-stick cooking spray. Alternately layer the cheese and bread in the insert, beginning and ending with bread.

2. In a small bowl, whisk the evaporated milk, eggs, and cayenne. Pour over the bread and cheese layers. Cook on low for 2–3 hours.

8 ounces reduced-fat sharp Cheddar, shredded

8 ounces skim-milk mozzarella, shredded

8 slices thin sandwich bread

2 cups fat-free evaporated milk

4 eggs

¼ teaspoon cayenne

Per Serving

Calories	Fat	Sodium	Carbohydrates	Fiber	Protein
310	16g	390mg	20g	0g	25g

Slow-Cooked Oatmeal with Dried and Fresh Fruit

SERVES 2

Place all ingredients in a 2-quart slow cooker. Cook on low for 8 hours. Stir prior to serving.

Per Serving

Calories	Fat	Sodium	Carbohydrates	Fiber	Protein
260	3g	0mg	52g	7g	6g

1 Bosc pear, peeled and cubed

1¼ cups water

¾ cup old-fashioned rolled oats

¼ cup dried tart cherries

¼ teaspoon sugar

¼ teaspoon ground ginger

Ham and Egg Casserole

Ham and Egg Casserole

1. In a small bowl, whisk the eggs, spices, Cheddar, and chiles. Stir in the ham. Set aside.

2. Spray a 2-quart slow cooker with nonstick cooking spray. Place the bread in a single layer on the bottom of the insert. Pour the egg mixture on top.

3. Cook on low for 7 hours. Use a spatula to separate the egg from the sides of the slow cooker. Lift the whole casserole out of the insert. Place it on a cutting board and slice it into six equal slices.

6 eggs

½ teaspoon freshly ground black pepper

¼ teaspoon paprika

⅓ cup shredded sharp Cheddar

4 ounces canned diced green chiles, drained

3 ounces 98% fat-free smoked ham slice, diced

2 slices thin sandwich bread

Per Serving

Calories	Fat	Sodium	Carbohydrates	Fiber	Protein
140	8g	410mg	5g	<1g	11g

Almond and Dried Cherry Granola

1. Place the oats and almonds in a 4-quart slow cooker. Drizzle with honey, oil, and vanilla. Stir the mixture to distribute the syrup evenly. Cook on high, uncovered, for 1½ hours, stirring every 15–20 minutes.

2. Add the cherries, coconut, and sunflower seeds. Reduce heat to low. Cook for 4 hours, uncovered, stirring every 20 minutes.

3. Allow the granola to cool fully, and then store it in an airtight container for up to 1 month.

5 cups old-fashioned rolled oats

1 cup slivered almonds

¼ cup mild honey

¼ cup canola oil

1 teaspoon vanilla

½ cup dried tart cherries

¼ cup unsweetened shredded coconut

½ cup sunflower seeds

Per Serving

Calories	Fat	Sodium	Carbohydrates	Fiber	Protein
180	8g	0mg	22g	4g	5g

Southwestern Casserole

In a 4-quart slow cooker, stir together all ingredients except the cheese. Cook on low for 8–9 hours. Stir in the cheese shortly before serving.

Per Serving

Calories	Fat	Sodium	Carbohydrates	Fiber	Protein
280	5g	550mg	46g	5g	15g

4 large red skin potatoes, diced

1½ cups cubed 98% fat-free hickory-smoked ham

1 large onion, diced

1 jalapeño, seeded and diced

1 tablespoon butter

15 ounces canned diced tomatoes

4 ounces sliced button mushrooms

¼ teaspoon salt

¼ teaspoon pepper

¼ cup shredded reduced-fat Cheddar or Mexican-blend cheese mix

Breakfast Burrito Filling

Place all ingredients in a 2-quart slow cooker. Stir. Cook on low for 8 hours. Stir before serving.

Per Serving

Calories	Fat	Sodium	Carbohydrates	Fiber	Protein
310	12g	430mg	6g	1g	44g

1¼ pounds lean boneless pork, cubed

12 ounces diced tomatoes with green chiles

1 small onion, diced

1 jalapeño, diced

½ teaspoon ground chipotle

¼ teaspoon cayenne

¼ teaspoon ground jalapeño

2 cloves garlic, minced

3

APPETIZERS AND BITES

Chicken Meatballs in a Hawaiian-Inspired Sauce

1. Preheat the oven to 375°F. Line 2 baking sheets with parchment paper. In a large bowl, use your hands to mix the chicken, ground ginger, 2 tablespoons of pineapple juice, bread crumbs, egg, and minced onions and garlic. Form into 1" balls. Place on the baking sheets and bake for 15 minutes or until cooked through.

2. Meanwhile, in a small bowl, whisk together the remaining pineapple juice, soy sauce, teriyaki sauce, ponzu sauce, lime juice, and cornstarch. Pour into a 6-quart slow cooker.

3. Add the grated ginger, sliced onions, pineapple, jalapeño, and brown sugar to the slow cooker. Stir.

4. Add the meatballs and cook on low for 6–9 hours.

2 pounds ground chicken breast

1 teaspoon ground ginger

¾ cup plus 2 tablespoons pineapple juice, divided use

½ cup bread crumbs

1 egg

¼ cup minced onion

2 cloves garlic, grated

¼ cup dark soy sauce

¼ cup teriyaki sauce

¼ cup ponzu sauce

3 tablespoons lime juice

1 tablespoon cornstarch

½ tablespoon grated fresh ginger

1 small onion, thinly sliced

4 cups cubed fresh pineapple

1 jalapeño, diced

⅓ cup brown sugar

Per Serving

Calories	Fat	Sodium	Carbohydrates	Fiber	Protein
170	5g	520mg	18g	1g	12g

Cinnamon and Sugar Peanuts

Place the peanuts in a 4-quart slow cooker. Add the cinnamon and sugar and drizzle with butter. Stir. Cook on low for 2–3 hours, uncovered, stirring occasionally.

12 ounces unsalted, roasted peanuts

½ tablespoon cinnamon

⅓ cup sugar

1 tablespoon melted butter

Per 1 ounce

Calories	Fat	Sodium	Carbohydrates	Fiber	Protein
200	15g	0mg	12g	2g	7g

Pineapple Teriyaki Drumsticks

Pineapple Teriyaki Drumsticks

1. Arrange the drumsticks in a single layer on a broiling pan. Broil for 10 minutes on high, flipping the drumsticks once halfway through the cooking time.

2. Drain the juice from the pineapple into a 4- or 6-quart oval slow cooker. Add the teriyaki sauce, ginger, and hoisin sauce. Stir to combine.

3. Cut the pineapple rings in half. Add them to the slow cooker.

4. Add the drumsticks to the slow cooker and stir to combine. Cover and cook on low for 4–6 hours.

12 chicken drumsticks

8 ounces canned pineapple slices in juice

¼ cup low-sodium teriyaki sauce

1 teaspoon ground ginger

¼ cup hoisin sauce

Per Serving

Calories	Fat	Sodium	Carbohydrates	Fiber	Protein
340	20g	300mg	6g	0g	31g

Hot and Spicy Nuts

1. Place the nuts in a 2- or 4-quart slow cooker. Drizzle with oil. Stir. Add the spices, and then stir again to distribute the seasoning evenly.

2. Cook on low for 1 hour, covered, then uncover and cook on low for 15 minutes or until the nuts look dry.

2½ cups skin-on almonds or mixed nuts

1 teaspoon canola oil

½ teaspoon ground jalapeño

½ teaspoon garlic powder

½ teaspoon cayenne

½ teaspoon ground chipotle

½ teaspoon paprika

¼ teaspoon salt

Per 1 ounce

Calories	Fat	Sodium	Carbohydrates	Fiber	Protein
170	15g	45mg	6g	3g	6g

Cranberry Turkey Meatballs

1. Defrost the meatballs according to package instructions. Mix together the chili sauce, Cranberry Sauce, brown sugar, and preserves in a large bowl.

2. Pour half of the sauce into the bottom of a 4-quart oval slow cooker. Place the meatballs on top. Pour the remaining sauce over the meatballs. Cook on low for 4 hours or on high for 2.

28 ounces frozen, precooked turkey meatballs (about 24 meatballs)

¼ cup chili sauce

3 cups Cranberry Sauce (Chapter 6)

1½ tablespoons dark brown sugar

1 tablespoon ginger preserves

Per Serving

Calories	Fat	Sodium	Carbohydrates	Fiber	Protein
120	4g	250mg	8g	0g	14g

Italian Turkey Meatballs

Italian Turkey Meatballs

1. Defrost the meatballs according to package instructions. Place them in a 2- or 4-quart slow cooker.

2. Heat the oil in a nonstick pan. Sauté the garlic, onions, and carrots until the onions and carrots start to soften. Add the crushed tomatoes, tomato paste, salt, pepper, and basil. Stir. Simmer until most of the liquid has evaporated.

3. Pour the sauce over the meatballs, and stir to coat them. Cook on low up to 6 hours. Garnish with parsley.

Per Serving

Calories	Fat	Sodium	Carbohydrates	Fiber	Protein
170	8g	250mg	13g	3g	11g

12 frozen Italian-style turkey meatballs

1 teaspoon canola oil

3 cloves garlic, minced

1 small onion, diced

1 carrot, diced

28 ounces canned crushed tomatoes

2 tablespoons tomato paste

⅛ teaspoon salt

½ teaspoon freshly ground black pepper

1 tablespoon minced fresh basil

1 tablespoon minced fresh parsley

Balsamic Almonds

1. Place all ingredients in a 4-quart oval slow cooker. Cook on high, uncovered, for 4 hours, stirring every 15 minutes or until all the liquid has evaporated. The almonds will have a syrupy coating.

2. Line two baking sheets with parchment paper. Pour the almonds in a single layer on the baking sheets to cool completely. Store in an airtight container for up to 1 week.

2 cups whole almonds
½ cup dark brown sugar
½ cup balsamic vinegar
½ teaspoon kosher salt

Per Serving

Calories	Fat	Sodium	Carbohydrates	Fiber	Protein
150	10g	80mg	14g	2g	4g

Sticky Honey Wings

1. Place the wings in an oval 4-quart slow cooker.
2. In a small bowl, whisk the honey, soy sauce, pepper, chili sauce, and garlic powder. Pour over the wings. Toss to coat with sauce.
3. Cook for 6–7 hours on low. Stir before serving.

3 pounds chicken wings, tips removed

¼ cup honey

¼ cup low-sodium soy sauce

½ teaspoon freshly ground black pepper

2 tablespoons chili sauce

½ teaspoon garlic powder

Per Serving

Calories	Fat	Sodium	Carbohydrates	Fiber	Protein
340	22g	290mg	8g	0g	25g

Green Curry Wings

1. Place the wings in a 4-quart oval slow cooker.
2. In a small bowl, whisk together the curry paste, basil, coconut milk, ginger, and cilantro. Pour the sauce over the wings. Toss the wings to coat.
3. Cook on low for 6 hours. Stir prior to serving.

3 pounds chicken wings, tips removed

8 ounces green curry paste

2 ounces Thai basil, minced

1 tablespoon light coconut milk

1 tablespoon minced fresh ginger

1 tablespoon minced fresh cilantro

Per Serving

Calories	Fat	Sodium	Carbohydrates	Fiber	Protein
320	23g	180mg	1g	0g	26g

Mango Pork Morsels

1. Quickly brown the pork in a nonstick skillet. Add the pork and mango to a 4-quart slow cooker.

2. In a small bowl, whisk together the garlic, jalapeño, salsa, salt, pepper, chipotle, chili powder, oregano, and the orange and lime juices. Pour over the mango and pork. Stir.

3. Cook on low for 6 hours; remove the cover and cook on high for 30 minutes. Stir before serving.

Per Serving

Calories	Fat	Sodium	Carbohydrates	Fiber	Protein
120	2.5g	105mg	9g	1g	15g

1½ pounds lean pork loin, cubed

2 mangoes, cubed

3 cloves garlic, minced

1 jalapeño, minced

1 tablespoon salsa

¼ teaspoon salt

¼ teaspoon freshly ground black pepper

2 teaspoons ground chipotle

1 teaspoon New Mexican chili powder

½ teaspoon oregano

2 tablespoons orange juice

2 tablespoons lime juice

Light and Creamy Swedish Meatballs

1. Preheat oven to 350°F. In a shallow saucepan, cook the bread and milk on low until the milk is absorbed, about 1 minute. Place the bread in a large bowl and add the meat, garlic, egg, ¼ teaspoon allspice, and ⅛ teaspoon nutmeg.

2. Mix until ingredients are evenly distributed. Roll into 1" balls. Line two baking sheets with parchment paper. Place the meatballs in a single layer on the baking sheets. Bake for 15 minutes, and then drain on paper towel–lined plates.

3. Meanwhile, bring the Chicken Stock, evaporated milk, butter, and remaining allspice and nutmeg to a simmer. Whisk in the flour and continue to whisk until the mixture is slightly thickened. Remove from heat.

4. Place the meatballs in a 4- or 6-quart oval slow cooker. Pour the sauce over the meatballs. Cook on low up to 6 hours. Stir gently before serving to distribute the sauce evenly.

2 thin slices white sandwich bread

½ cup 1% milk

2 pounds 94% lean ground beef or ground chicken

2 cloves garlic, minced

1 egg

½ teaspoon allspice, divided use

¼ teaspoon nutmeg, divided use

3 cups Chicken Stock (Chapter 4)

12 ounces fat-free evaporated milk

1 tablespoon melted butter

⅓ cup all-purpose flour

Per Serving

Calories	Fat	Sodium	Carbohydrates	Fiber	Protein
110	3.5g	125mg	7g	0g	13g

Caramelized Onion Dip

1. Place all ingredients in a 1½- or 2-quart slow cooker.

2. Heat on low for 2 hours. Whisk before serving.

Per 2 tablespoons

Calories	Fat	Sodium	Carbohydrates	Fiber	Protein
30	1.5g	35mg	3g	0g	1g

⅔ cup Caramelized Onions (Chapter 5)

8 ounces reduced-fat cream cheese

8 ounces reduced-fat or fat-free sour cream

1 tablespoon Worcestershire sauce

¼ teaspoon white pepper

⅛ teaspoon flour

Stuffed Grape Leaves

Stuffed Grape Leaves

1. Prepare the grape leaves according to package instructions. Set aside.

2. Spray a nonstick skillet with cooking spray. Sauté the meat and shallot until the meat is thoroughly cooked. Drain off any excess fat. Scrape into a bowl and add the rice, dill, ¼ cup of the lemon juice, parsley, mint, fennel seed, pepper, and salt. Stir to incorporate all ingredients.

3. Place a leaf, stem-side up, with the top of the leaf pointing away from you on a clean work surface. Place 1 teaspoon filling in the middle of the leaf. Fold the bottom toward the middle and then fold in the sides. Roll it toward the top to seal. Repeat.

4. Place the rolled grape leaves in two or three layers in a 4-quart oval slow cooker. Pour in the water and remaining lemon juice. Cover and cook on low for 4–6 hours. Serve warm or cold.

16 ounces jarred grape leaves (about 60 leaves)

¾ pound 94% lean ground beef, chicken, or pork

1 shallot, minced

¾ cup cooked brown or white rice

¼ cup minced fresh dill

½ cup lemon juice, divided use

2 tablespoons minced fresh parsley

1 tablespoon dried mint

1 tablespoon fennel seed

¼ teaspoon freshly ground black pepper

⅛ teaspoon salt

2 cups water

Per Serving

Calories	Fat	Sodium	Carbohydrates	Fiber	Protein
30	1g	20mg	3g	<1g	3g

Baba Ganoush

1. Pierce the eggplant with a fork. Cook on high in a 4-quart slow cooker for 2 hours.

2. Allow to cool. Peel off the skin. Slice in half and remove the seeds. Discard the skin and seeds.

3. Place the pulp in a food processor and add the remaining ingredients. Pulse until smooth.

1 (1-pound) eggplant
2 tablespoons tahini
2 tablespoons lemon juice
2 cloves garlic

Per Serving

Calories	Fat	Sodium	Carbohydrates	Fiber	Protein
25	1.5g	0mg	3g	2g	1g

Slow-Cooked Salsa

1. Place all ingredients in a 2-quart slow cooker. Stir. Cook on low for 5 hours.

2. Stir and lightly smash the tomatoes before serving, if desired.

4 cups grape tomatoes, halved
1 small onion, thinly sliced
2 jalapeños, diced
⅛ teaspoon salt

Per Serving

Calories	Fat	Sodium	Carbohydrates	Fiber	Protein
20	0g	35mg	4g	1g	1g

Broccoli Dip

1. Place the broccoli, spinach, shallot, jalapeño, Worcestershire sauce, and capers in a food processor. Pulse until the mixture is mostly smooth. Add the yogurt, pepper, and lemon juice. Pulse until smooth.

2. Pour into a 1½- or 2-quart slow cooker. Cover and cook on low for 1 hour.

4 cups steamed broccoli florets

1 cup fresh baby spinach

1 shallot

1 jalapeño, stem and seeds removed

1 tablespoon Worcestershire sauce

½ tablespoon nonpareil capers

1 cup nonfat plain yogurt

¼ teaspoon freshly ground black pepper

2 tablespoons lemon juice

Per Serving

Calories	Fat	Sodium	Carbohydrates	Fiber	Protein
20	0g	40mg	4g	<1g	2g

Creamy Low-Fat Spinach-Artichoke Dip

Creamy Low-Fat Spinach-Artichoke Dip

SERVES 15

1. Heat the oil in a nonstick skillet. Sauté the onions, artichoke hearts, and spinach until the onions are translucent and the spinach wilts. Drain any extra liquid.

2. Place in a 2-quart slow cooker. Stir in sour cream, Worcestershire sauce, salt, pepper, and cheese.

3. Cover and cook on low for 1 hour. Stir before serving.

Per Serving

Calories	Fat	Sodium	Carbohydrates	Fiber	Protein
35	2g	95mg	3g	1g	2g

½ teaspoon canola oil

½ cup diced yellow onion

¼ cup diced red onion

8 ounces frozen artichoke hearts, defrosted

3 ounces baby spinach

6 ounces reduced-fat sour cream

1 tablespoon Worcestershire sauce

¼ teaspoon salt

½ teaspoon freshly ground black pepper

⅓ cup reduced-fat Italian-blend cheese

Shrimp and Artichoke Dip

SERVES 20

1. Place the cream cheese, sour cream, green onions, Worcestershire sauce, and Chesapeake Bay seasoning in a food processor. Pulse until smooth and well blended. Add the artichoke hearts and pulse twice.

2. Scrape into a medium bowl. Add the shrimp and stir to evenly distribute.

3. Scrape into a 2-quart slow cooker. Cook on low for 40 minutes. Stir before serving.

8 ounces reduced-fat cream cheese

½ cup reduced-fat sour cream

½ cup diced green onion

1 tablespoon Worcestershire sauce

1½ teaspoons Chesapeake Bay seasoning

12 ounces frozen artichoke hearts, defrosted

8 ounces peeled salad shrimp

Per Serving

Calories	Fat	Sodium	Carbohydrates	Fiber	Protein
50	3g	220mg	3g	<1g	4g

Sun-Dried Tomato and Pesto Dip

SERVES 20

1. Place the garlic, mayonnaise, basil, pine nuts, and pepper in a food processor. Pulse until a fairly smooth paste forms. Add the sun-dried tomatoes and pulse 4–5 times. Add the cream cheese and pulse until smooth.

2. Scrape into a 2-quart slow cooker. Cook on low for 1 hour. Stir before serving.

Per Serving

Calories	Fat	Sodium	Carbohydrates	Fiber	Protein
35	3g	65mg	1g	0g	1g

2 cloves garlic

1 tablespoon reduced-fat mayonnaise

¾ ounce fresh basil

1 teaspoon toasted pine nuts

¼ teaspoon white pepper

¼ cup julienne-cut dry (not oil-packed) sun-dried tomatoes

8 ounces reduced-fat cream cheese or Neufchâtel, at room temperature

Hummus

1. Place the chickpeas in a 4-quart slow cooker and cover with water. Soak overnight. The next day, cook on low for 8 hours.

2. Drain, reserving the liquid. Place the chickpeas, tahini, lemon juice, garlic, and salt in a food processor. Pulse until smooth, adding the reserved liquid as needed to achieve the desired texture. Serve with pita bread and vegetables.

1 pound dried chickpeas

Water, as needed

3 tablespoons tahini

3 tablespoons lemon juice

3 cloves garlic

¼ teaspoon salt

Per Serving

Calories	Fat	Sodium	Carbohydrates	Fiber	Protein
40	1.5g	100mg	6g	1g	2g

Summer Fruit Dip

In a small bowl, whisk together all ingredients. Pour into a 2-quart slow cooker. Cook on low for 1 hour. Stir before serving.

½ cup raspberry purée

8 ounces reduced-fat cream cheese, at room temperature

1 tablespoon sugar

¾ cup reduced-fat sour cream

1 teaspoon vanilla

Per Serving

Calories	Fat	Sodium	Carbohydrates	Fiber	Protein
45	3g	40mg	3g	0g	2g

Hummus

STOCKS, SOUPS, AND CHILIS

4

Chicken Stock

1. Place the carcass, wings, carrots, celery, onions, parsnips, and garlic in a 6-quart slow cooker.

2. Fill the slow cooker with water until it is 2" below the top. Cover and cook on low for 10 hours.

3. Strain into a large container. Discard the solids. Refrigerate the stock overnight.

4. The next day, scoop off any fat that has floated to the top. Discard the fat.

5. Freeze or refrigerate the stock until ready to use.

1 chicken carcass plus 2 chicken wings

2 carrots, cut into chunks

2 stalks celery, cut into chunks

2 onions, cut into chunks

2 parsnips, cut into chunks

1 whole head garlic

Water, as needed

Per 1 cup

Calories	Fat	Sodium	Carbohydrates	Fiber	Protein
60	1.5g	25mg	10g	2g	3g

Roasted Vegetable Stock

1. Preheat oven to 425°F. Arrange the vegetables and herbs in a 9" × 13" baking pan lined with parchment paper. Roast for 30 minutes or until browned.

2. Add the vegetables to a 6-quart slow cooker. Add 5 quarts of water and cover. Cook on low for 8–10 hours. Strain the stock, discarding the solids. Freeze or refrigerate the stock until ready to use.

Per 1 cup

Calories	Fat	Sodium	Carbohydrates	Fiber	Protein
100	0g	45mg	24g	5g	3g

3 carrots

3 parsnips

3 large onions, quartered

3 whole turnips

3 rutabagas, quartered

3 bell peppers, halved

2 shallots

1 whole head garlic

1 bunch fresh thyme

1 bunch fresh parsley

5 quarts water

Spicy Smoked Turkey Stock

1. Place all ingredients in a 4-quart slow cooker. Cook on low for 10 hours.

2. Strain the liquid through a fine-mesh sieve, and discard the solids. Refrigerate overnight.

3. The next day, skim off any fat that has floated to the surface. Refrigerate or freeze the stock until needed.

Per 1 cup

Calories	Fat	Sodium	Carbohydrates	Fiber	Protein
90	3.5g	330mg	4g	<1g	10g

2 smoked turkey drumsticks

5 dried guajillo chiles, stems and seeds removed

5 dried pasilla chiles, stems and seeds removed

6 dried red chiles, stems and seeds removed

3½ quarts water

1 large onion, quartered

3 cloves garlic

Fish Stock

1. Place all ingredients in a 4-quart slow cooker. Cook on low for 8–10 hours.

2. Remove all the solids. Refrigerate overnight. The next day, skim off any foam. Use, refrigerate, or freeze the stock.

3 quarts water

2 onions, quartered

Head and bones from 3 fishes, any type

2 stalks celery, chopped

2 tablespoons peppercorns

1 bunch parsley

Per 1 cup

Calories	Fat	Sodium	Carbohydrates	Fiber	Protein
35	1g	10mg	3g	1g	4g

Gumbo

Gumbo

1. In a nonstick skillet, melt the butter. Add the flour and stir until the flour is golden brown. Add the pepper, garlic, onions, carrots, and celery. Sauté for 1 minute.

2. Add the mixture to a 4-quart slow cooker. Add the Chicken Stock, seasoning, chicken breast, and tomatoes. Cook on low for 8–10 hours.

3. Add the okra for the last hour of cooking. Garnish with scallions. Serve with rice for a complete meal.

2 tablespoons butter

2 tablespoons flour

1 Cubanelle pepper, diced

4 cloves garlic, diced

1 onion, diced

2 carrots, diced

2 stalks celery, diced

1 quart Chicken Stock (recipe in this chapter)

2 tablespoons Cajun seasoning

12 ounces chicken breast

1½ cups diced fresh tomatoes

2 cups diced okra

1 tablespoon minced scallions

Per Serving

Calories	Fat	Sodium	Carbohydrates	Fiber	Protein
130	6g	680mg	14g	3g	6g

Mushroom Barley Soup

1. Place the dried porcini mushrooms in a heat-safe bowl. Pour the boiling water over the mushrooms. Soak for 15 minutes.

2. Meanwhile, melt the butter in a medium skillet. Sauté the fresh mushrooms, onions, and garlic until the onions are soft.

3. Drain the porcini mushrooms and discard the water. Add all of the mushrooms, onions, garlic, barley, pepper, and broth to a 4-quart slow cooker. Stir. Cook on low for 6–8 hours.

1 ounce dried porcini mushrooms

1 cup boiling water

1½ teaspoons butter

5 ounces sliced fresh shiitake mushrooms

4 ounces sliced fresh button mushrooms

1 large onion, diced

1 clove garlic, minced

⅔ cup medium pearl barley

¼ teaspoon freshly ground black pepper

6 cups beef broth

Per Serving

Calories	Fat	Sodium	Carbohydrates	Fiber	Protein
110	1.5g	590mg	20g	4g	6g

Hot and Sour Soup

Place all ingredients in a 4-quart slow cooker. Stir. Cook on low for 8 hours or on high for 3½ hours.

Per Serving

Calories	Fat	Sodium	Carbohydrates	Fiber	Protein
90	3g	770mg	10g	2g	8g

4 cups Chicken Stock or Roasted Vegetable Stock (recipes in this chapter)

15 ounces canned straw mushrooms, drained

7 ounces cubed extra-firm tofu

6 ounces canned bamboo shoots, drained

3 tablespoons rice vinegar

2 tablespoons Chinese black vinegar

1 tablespoon garlic-chili sauce

3 tablespoons dark soy sauce

1 teaspoon freshly ground black pepper

1 teaspoon white pepper

½ teaspoon sesame oil

½ teaspoon hot chile oil

¾ cup snow peas

Tortilla Soup

1. Place the spices, tomatoes, stock, garlic, onions, and peppers in a 4-quart slow cooker. Cover and cook on low for 6 hours.

2. After 6 hours, add the corn and chicken or turkey. Cover and cook for an additional 45–60 minutes.

Per Serving

Calories	Fat	Sodium	Carbohydrates	Fiber	Protein
170	3g	350mg	21g	4g	17g

1 teaspoon cumin

1 teaspoon chili powder

1 teaspoon smoked paprika

⅛ teaspoon salt

25 ounces canned crushed tomatoes

14 ounces canned fire-roasted diced tomatoes

3 cups Chicken Stock or Spicy Smoked Turkey Stock (recipes in this chapter)

2 cloves garlic, minced

1 medium onion, diced

4 ounces canned diced green chiles, drained

2 habanero peppers, diced

1 cup fresh corn kernels

2 cups cubed cooked chicken or turkey breast

Greek-Style Orzo and Spinach Soup

SERVES 6

1. Add the garlic, lemon juice, zest, Chicken Stock, and onions to a 4-quart slow cooker. Cover and cook on low for 6–8 hours.

2. Stir in the chicken and cook on high for 30 minutes. Add the orzo and spinach. Stir and continue to cook on high for an additional 15 minutes. Stir before serving.

2 cloves garlic, minced

3 tablespoons lemon juice

1 teaspoon lemon zest

5 cups Chicken Stock (recipe in this chapter)

1 small onion, thinly sliced

1 cup cubed cooked chicken breast

⅓ cup dried orzo

4 cups fresh baby spinach

Per Serving

Calories	Fat	Sodium	Carbohydrates	Fiber	Protein
150	3.5g	330mg	16g	1g	14g

Pumpkin Bisque

Pumpkin Bisque

1. Place puréed pumpkin, water, evaporated milk, nutmeg, garlic, and onions in a 4-quart slow cooker. Stir. Cook on low for 8 hours.

2. Use an immersion blender or blend the bisque in batches in a standard blender until smooth. Garnish with sage and serve hot.

2 cups puréed pumpkin

4 cups water

1 cup fat-free evaporated milk

¼ teaspoon nutmeg

2 cloves garlic, minced

1 onion, minced

1 tablespoon sage

Per Serving

Calories	Fat	Sodium	Carbohydrates	Fiber	Protein
110	0.5g	80mg	21g	4g	7g

Posole

1. Seed the chiles, reserving the seeds. In a dry, hot frying pan, heat the chiles until warmed through and fragrant. Do not burn or brown them. Place the chiles and seeds in a medium pot with 1 quart Chicken Stock or water, garlic, lime juice, cumin, and oregano. Bring to a boil and continue to boil for 20 minutes.

2. Meanwhile, in a plastic bag, toss the cubed pork with the flour to coat. Heat the oil in a large nonstick skillet and brown the meat on all sides. Add the onions and cook about 5 minutes or until the onions are soft.

3. Pour the remaining stock or water, hominy, and the onion and pork mixture into a 4-quart slow cooker.

4. Strain the chile-stock mixture through a mesh sieve into the slow cooker insert, mashing down with a wooden spoon to press out the pulp and juice. Discard the seeds and remaining solids.

5. Cook on low for 8 hours.

8 large dried New Mexican red chiles

1½ quarts Chicken Stock (recipe in this chapter) or water, divided use

3 cloves garlic, minced

2 tablespoons lime juice

1 tablespoon cumin

1 tablespoon oregano

2 pounds boneless pork loin, cubed

¾ cup flour

1 teaspoon canola oil

1 large onion, sliced

40 ounces canned hominy

Per Serving

Calories	Fat	Sodium	Carbohydrates	Fiber	Protein
370	8g	480mg	37g	7g	36g

Tlalpeño Soup

1. Heat the oil on a nonstick skillet. Sauté the onions, carrots, and celery until the onions are translucent and the carrots are slightly softened.

2. Place the sautéed vegetables, both kinds of chiles, chickpeas, adobo, and Chicken Stock in a 4-quart slow cooker. Stir. Cook on low up to 9 hours.

3. About 30–40 minutes before serving, stir in the chicken, and cook on high.

1 teaspoon canola oil

1 small onion, diced

2 carrots, diced

2 stalks celery, diced

4 ounces canned green chiles

2 chipotle chiles in adobo, minced

15 ounces canned chickpeas, drained

1 tablespoon adobo, from the can of chipotle chiles in adobo

6 cups Chicken Stock (recipe in this chapter)

3 cups diced cooked chicken

Per Serving

Calories	Fat	Sodium	Carbohydrates	Fiber	Protein
250	6g	1,130mg	24g	4g	24g

Rosemary-Thyme Stew

1. Heat the oil in a large skillet. Sauté the onions, flour, carrots, celery, garlic, potatoes, thyme, rosemary, and chicken until the chicken is white on all sides. Drain off any excess fat.

2. Put sautéed ingredients into a 4-quart slow cooker. Sprinkle with salt and pepper. Pour in the water or Chicken Stock. Stir. Cook on low for 8–9 hours.

3. Add the corn. Cover and cook on high for an additional ½ hour. Stir before serving.

Per Serving

Calories	Fat	Sodium	Carbohydrates	Fiber	Protein
260	6g	270mg	14g	3g	37g

1 teaspoon canola oil

1 large onion, diced

1 tablespoon flour

1 carrot, diced

2 stalks celery, diced

2 cloves garlic, minced

1 cup diced Yukon Gold potatoes

3½ tablespoons minced fresh thyme

3 tablespoons minced fresh rosemary

1 pound boneless skinless chicken breast, cut into 1" cubes

¼ teaspoon salt

½ teaspoon freshly ground black pepper

1½ cup water or Chicken Stock (recipe in this chapter)

½ cup frozen or fresh corn kernels

Turkey White Chili

Place all ingredients except the turkey in a 2-quart slow cooker. Stir to mix the ingredients. Cook on low for 8 hours; stir in the turkey. Cook on high for an additional 30–60 minutes.

Per Serving

Calories	Fat	Sodium	Carbohydrates	Fiber	Protein
110	1.5g	170mg	11g	2g	12g

¼ cup drained canned hominy

¼ cup cooked or canned cannellini beans, drained and rinsed

¼ cup onions, diced

1 teaspoon lemon juice

½ teaspoon cumin

½ teaspoon paprika

½ teaspoon white pepper

2 ounces drained canned green peppers

½ cooked turkey breast, cubed

Pho

Pho

1. Quickly heat the spices, ginger, and onions in a dry non-stick skillet until the seeds start to pop. The onions and ginger should look slightly caramelized. Place them in a cheesecloth packet and tie it securely.

2. Fill a large pot with water. Bring the water to a boil and add the beef knuckles. Boil for 10 minutes. Remove from the heat and skim off the foam that rises to the surface.

3. Place the bones and the cheesecloth packet in a 6- or 7-quart slow cooker. Add the stock and fill the slow cooker with water to 1" below the top. Cook on low for up to 10 hours or overnight. Strain off any solids. Remove the bones and the packet.

4. Add the sliced beef and noodles. Cook on low for about 15 minutes or until the beef is cooked and the noodles are tender.

5. Garnish each bowl with cilantro, basil, and sprouts.

1 tablespoon coriander seeds

1 tablespoon whole cloves

6 star anise

1 cinnamon stick

1 tablespoon fennel seed

1 tablespoon whole cardamom

4" knob peeled fresh ginger, sliced

1 onion, sliced

Water, as needed

3 pounds beef knuckles or oxtails

1 quart beef stock

¾ pound thinly sliced lean beef

8 ounces Vietnamese rice noodles

½ cup chopped cilantro

½ cup chopped Thai basil

2 cups mung bean sprouts

Per Serving

Calories	Fat	Sodium	Carbohydrates	Fiber	Protein
270	3.5g	110mg	41g	3g	19g

Curried Cauliflower Soup

1. Place all ingredients in a 4-quart slow cooker. Stir. Cook on low for 8 hours.
2. Use an immersion blender or blend the soup in batches in a standard blender until smooth.

1 pound cauliflower florets

2½ cups water

1 onion, minced

2 cloves garlic, minced

3 teaspoons curry powder

¼ teaspoon cumin

Per Serving

Calories	Fat	Sodium	Carbohydrates	Fiber	Protein
60	0g	40mg	11g	4g	4g

Leek, Potato, and Carrot Potage

1. Place all ingredients in a 4-quart slow cooker. Cook on low for 7 hours.
2. Purée using an immersion blender or purée in batches in a standard blender. Serve piping hot.

4 cups sliced leeks

4 russet potatoes, peeled and cubed

2 carrots, diced

5 cups water

¼ teaspoon salt

½ teaspoon white pepper

Per Serving

Calories	Fat	Sodium	Carbohydrates	Fiber	Protein
160	0g	130mg	36g	4g	4g

Cioppino

1. Place the chopped onions, celery, garlic, tomatoes, clam juice, water or Fish Stock, tomato paste, red pepper flakes, oregano, parsley, and vinegar in a 4-quart slow cooker. Stir vigorously. Cook on low for 8 hours.

2. Add the seafood and green onions and cook on high for 30 minutes. Stir prior to serving.

Per Serving

Calories	Fat	Sodium	Carbohydrates	Fiber	Protein
210	5g	510mg	13g	3g	30g

1 onion, chopped

2 stalks celery, diced

6 cloves garlic, minced

28 ounces canned diced tomatoes

8 ounces clam juice

¾ cup water or Fish Stock (recipe in this chapter)

6 ounces tomato paste

1 teaspoon red pepper flakes

2 tablespoons minced fresh oregano

2 tablespoons minced fresh Italian parsley

1 teaspoon red wine vinegar

10 ounces catfish nuggets

10 ounces peeled raw shrimp

6 ounces diced cooked clams

6 ounces lump crabmeat

¾ cup diced lobster meat

¼ cup diced green onion

Winter Vegetable Soup

Place all ingredients except the dill in a 2-quart slow cooker. Stir. Cook on low for 8 hours. Garnish with dill and serve hot.

Per Serving

Calories	Fat	Sodium	Carbohydrates	Fiber	Protein
210	3.5g	610mg	38g	6g	10g

1 small carrot, diced

1 stalk celery, diced

1 parsnip, diced

¼ cup cubed celeriac

¼ cup canned diced tomatoes

1 clove garlic, minced

1 shallot, minced

2 cups Chicken Stock (recipe in this chapter)

1 teaspoon celery flakes

¼ teaspoon white pepper

⅛ teaspoon salt

1 tablespoon fresh dill

Winter Vegetable Soup

Fiery Chicken Chili

1. Quickly sauté the ground chicken in a nonstick skillet until just cooked through. Drain all fat.
2. Place all ingredients in a 4-quart slow cooker. Stir. Cook on low for 8–10 hours.

Per Serving

Calories	Fat	Sodium	Carbohydrates	Fiber	Protein
210	5g	550mg	30g	11g	17g

1 pound ground chicken

3 cloves garlic, chopped

3 chipotle chiles in adobo

15 ounces canned dark red kidney beans, drained and rinsed

15 ounces canned black beans, drained and rinsed

1 teaspoon Worcestershire sauce

30 ounces canned diced tomatoes

4 ounces canned diced green chiles

1 teaspoon cayenne

1 teaspoon ground chipotle

1 onion, chopped

1 tablespoon habanero hot sauce

1 teaspoon paprika

1 teaspoon hot chili powder

1 teaspoon liquid smoke

Smoky Chipotle Pork Chili

1. Quickly sauté the pork in a nonstick skillet until just cooked through. Drain off any fat.
2. Place all ingredients in a 4-quart slow cooker. Stir. Cook on low for 8–10 hours.

Per Serving

Calories	Fat	Sodium	Carbohydrates	Fiber	Protein
270	13g	580mg	25g	9g	17g

1 pound ground pork

30 ounces canned fire-roasted diced tomatoes

3 chipotle chiles in adobo, chopped

1 teaspoon liquid smoke

1 teaspoon chili powder

1 teaspoon ground chipotle

1 teaspoon hot paprika

1 teaspoon smoked paprika

30 ounces canned chili beans, drained and rinsed

1 medium onion, diced

3 cloves garlic, minced

Acorn Squash Chili

1. Place all ingredients except the corn in a 4-quart slow cooker. Cook on low for 8 hours.

2. Add the corn and stir. Cover and continue to cook on low for ½ hour. Stir before serving.

Per Serving

Calories	Fat	Sodium	Carbohydrates	Fiber	Protein
170	0.5g	390mg	35g	10g	7g

2 cups cubed acorn squash

30 ounces canned petite diced tomatoes

2 stalks celery, diced

1 medium onion, diced

3 cloves garlic, minced

2 carrots, diced

1 teaspoon mesquite liquid smoke

2 teaspoons hot sauce

1 teaspoon chili powder

1 teaspoon paprika

1 teaspoon oregano

1 teaspoon smoked paprika

15 ounces canned kidney beans, drained and rinsed

15 ounces canned cannellini beans, drained and rinsed

1 cup fresh corn kernels

Three Bean Chili

1. Place all ingredients except the corn in a 4-quart slow cooker. Cook on low for 8 hours.

2. Add the corn and stir. Cover and continue to cook on low for ½ hour. Stir before serving.

Per Serving

Calories	Fat	Sodium	Carbohydrates	Fiber	Protein
180	1.5g	630mg	39g	11g	9g

1 teaspoon minced fresh jalapeño

30 ounces canned diced tomatoes

2 stalks celery, diced

1 medium onion, diced

3 cloves garlic, minced

2 carrots, diced

1 teaspoon cayenne

1 teaspoon chili powder

1 teaspoon paprika

1 teaspoon cumin

2 teaspoons jalapeño hot sauce

15 ounces canned black beans, drained and rinsed

15 ounces canned kidney beans, drained and rinsed

15 ounces canned cannellini beans, drained and rinsed

1 cup fresh corn kernels

Lean Green Chili

Place all ingredients except the chicken in a 4-quart slow cooker. Cook on low for 8 hours. Stir in the chicken, put the lid back on, and cook on low for an additional hour. Stir before serving.

Per Serving

Calories	Fat	Sodium	Carbohydrates	Fiber	Protein
190	3g	320mg	25g	7g	17g

30 ounces canned cannellini beans, drained and rinsed

1 teaspoon cumin

1 teaspoon ground jalapeño

1 jalapeño, minced

2 cloves garlic, minced

4 ounces canned green chiles, drained

28 ounces canned tomatillos, drained

1 medium onion, diced

1 tablespoon lime juice

1 teaspoon celery flakes

1 stalk celery, diced

2 cups diced cooked chicken breast

86 THE NEW SLOW COOKER COOKBOOK

Spicy Sausage Chili

1. Brown the sausage in a nonstick skillet. Drain off all fat.

2. Add the sausage and remaining ingredients to a 4-quart slow cooker and stir to combine and break up the hominy as needed. Cook on low for 8–10 hours.

1½ pounds spicy chicken sausage

2 teaspoons cayenne

1 tablespoon ground chipotle

1 teaspoon hot paprika

1 teaspoon hot chili powder

15 ounces canned cannellini beans, drained and rinsed

15 ounces canned tomatoes with green chiles

15 ounces canned hominy

1 teaspoon cumin

Per Serving

Calories	Fat	Sodium	Carbohydrates	Fiber	Protein
270	15g	1,240mg	18g	4g	14g

Turkey-Tomatillo Chili

SERVES 8

Place all ingredients except the turkey in a 4-quart slow cooker. Stir to mix the ingredients. Cook on low for 8 hours, and then stir in the turkey. Cook on high for an additional 30–60 minutes.

Per Serving

Calories	Fat	Sodium	Carbohydrates	Fiber	Protein
170	2g	390mg	22g	9g	17g

2 cups cubed tomatillos

1 green bell pepper, diced

1 onion, diced

1 teaspoon cayenne

1 teaspoon cumin

1 teaspoon paprika

1 teaspoon chili powder

30 ounces canned chili beans, drained and rinsed

2 cups cubed cooked turkey breast

Turkey-Tomatillo Chili

California Chili

1. Place all ingredients except the chicken in a 4-quart slow cooker. Cook on low for 8 hours.

2. Stir in the chicken, cover the cooker again, and cook on low for an additional hour. Stir before serving.

Per Serving

Calories	Fat	Sodium	Carbohydrates	Fiber	Protein
200	2.5g	570mg	25g	5g	18g

15 ounces hominy

15 ounces fire-roasted tomatoes with garlic

½ cup canned cannellini beans, drained and rinsed

1 teaspoon cumin

1 teaspoon ground jalapeño

2 Anaheim chiles, diced

6 cloves garlic, thinly sliced

1 medium onion, diced

1 stalk celery, diced

1 tablespoon lime juice

1 teaspoon ground chipotle

1 teaspoon California chili powder

2 cups diced cooked chicken breast

Summer Chili

1. Sauté the chicken in a nonstick pan until just browned. Add to a 4-quart slow cooker along with the fennel, radishes, celery, carrots, onions, shallots, garlic, habanero, beans, tomato paste, and all spices. Stir.
2. Cook on low for 6–7 hours. Then stir in the zucchini, tomatoes, and corn. Cook on high for an additional 30 minutes. Stir before serving.

Per Serving

Calories	Fat	Sodium	Carbohydrates	Fiber	Protein
200	3.5g	520mg	35g	9g	12g

½ pound ground chicken

1 bulb fennel, diced

4 radishes, diced

2 stalks celery, diced, including leaves

2 carrots, cut into coin-sized pieces

1 medium onion, diced

1 shallot, diced

4 cloves garlic, sliced

1 habanero pepper, diced

15 ounces canned cannellini beans, drained and rinsed

12 ounces tomato paste

½ teaspoon dried oregano

½ teaspoon black pepper

½ teaspoon crushed rosemary

½ teaspoon cayenne

½ teaspoon ground chipotle

1 teaspoon chili powder

1 teaspoon tarragon

¼ teaspoon cumin

¼ teaspoon celery seed

2 zucchini, cubed

10 Campari tomatoes, quartered

1 cup corn kernels

Mushroom Chili

Place all ingredients in a 4-quart slow cooker. Stir. Cook on low for 8 hours.

Per Serving

Calories	Fat	Sodium	Carbohydrates	Fiber	Protein
120	1.5g	740mg	29g	9g	8g

3 Portobello mushrooms, cubed

15 ounces canned black beans, drained and rinsed

1 onion, diced

3 cloves garlic, sliced

2½ cups diced fresh tomatoes

1 chipotle pepper in adobo, minced

½ teaspoon jalapeño hot sauce

1 teaspoon cumin

½ teaspoon cayenne

½ teaspoon freshly ground black pepper

¼ teaspoon salt

Super-Mild Chili

1. Brown the turkey in a nonstick skillet. Drain if needed.
2. Add the turkey and all of the remaining ingredients to a 4-quart slow cooker. Stir. Cook on low for 7–8 hours. Stir before serving.

Per Serving

Calories	Fat	Sodium	Carbohydrates	Fiber	Protein
280	7g	550mg	34g	9g	21g

1 pound ground turkey

30 ounces canned cannellini beans, drained and rinsed

28 ounces canned crushed tomatoes

1 teaspoon oregano

½ teaspoon cumin

1 teaspoon mild chili powder

1 bell pepper, diced

1 Vidalia onion, diced

2 cloves garlic, minced

Texas Firehouse Chili

1. Quickly brown the beef in a nonstick skillet. Drain off any excess grease.

2. Add the meat and all of the remaining ingredients to a 4-quart slow cooker. Cook on low up to 10 hours.

1 pound cubed lean beef

2 tablespoons onion powder

1 tablespoon garlic powder

2 tablespoons Mexican-style chili powder

1 tablespoon paprika

½ teaspoon oregano

½ teaspoon freshly ground black pepper

½ teaspoon white pepper

½ teaspoon cayenne pepper

½ teaspoon ground chipotle

8 ounces tomato sauce

Per Serving

Calories	Fat	Sodium	Carbohydrates	Fiber	Protein
260	12g	430mg	12g	3g	25g

Filipino-Influenced Pork Chili

1. Sauté the cubed pork in a dry skillet for 5 minutes. Drain off any fat.
2. Add the pork and remaining ingredients to a 4-quart slow cooker. Stir. Cook on low for 8 hours. Stir before serving.

Per Serving

Calories	Fat	Sodium	Carbohydrates	Fiber	Protein
210	2.5g	70mg	36g	4g	14g

1 pound pork loin, cubed

1½ cups canned crushed tomatoes

⅓ cup banana sauce

2 tablespoons lime juice

2 tablespoons cane vinegar

1 teaspoon ginger juice

1 teaspoon chili powder

½ teaspoon freshly ground black pepper

2 jarred pimentos, minced

1 onion, minced

3 unripe plantains, diced

2 tomatoes, cubed

1 large sweet potato, cubed

VEGETABLES AND SIDES

Stewed Squash

1. Place the onions on the bottom of a 1½- or 2-quart slow cooker. Top with zucchini, dill, lemon juice, salt, and pepper. Cook on low for 3½ hours.

2. Add the corn and butter and stir. Cook on high for an additional 30 minutes.

1 medium onion, cut into ¼" slices
3 cups sliced zucchini
1 tablespoon minced fresh dill
3 tablespoons lemon juice
¼ teaspoon salt
¼ teaspoon black pepper
¾ cup fresh corn kernels
1 teaspoon butter

Per Serving

Calories	Fat	Sodium	Carbohydrates	Fiber	Protein
70	1.5g	160mg	14g	2g	2g

Garlic Mashed Potatoes

1. Place the potatoes in a 4-quart slow cooker. Add garlic, Chicken Stock, and parsley. Stir. Cover and cook on high until potatoes are tender, about 3–4 hours.

2. Pour in milk, butter, and sour cream. Mash with a potato masher.

3 pounds red skin potatoes, quartered
4 cloves garlic, minced
¾ cup Chicken Stock (Chapter 4)
1 tablespoon minced fresh parsley
¼ cup 1% milk
1 tablespoon butter
⅓ cup reduced-fat sour cream

Per Serving

Calories	Fat	Sodium	Carbohydrates	Fiber	Protein
130	2.5g	50mg	23g	2g	4g

Garlic Mashed Potatoes

Slimmed-Down Macaroni and Cheese

1. Spray a 4-quart slow cooker with nonstick cooking spray. In a small saucepan, heat the mustard, cornstarch, pepper, and evaporated milk until warmed through, whisking occasionally. Stir in the cheese.

2. Pour the macaroni into the slow cooker. Top with the cheese mixture and stir. Cover and cook on low for 1–2 hours or on high for 30 minutes.

1 teaspoon dry mustard

2 tablespoons cornstarch

¼ teaspoon freshly ground black pepper

2½ cups fat-free evaporated milk

1½ cups shredded reduced-fat sharp Cheddar

8 ounces cooked macaroni

Per Serving

Calories	Fat	Sodium	Carbohydrates	Fiber	Protein
230	7g	125mg	26g	<1g	17g

Salt-Baked Potatoes

1. Pour about ½" of salt into the bottom of an oval 4-quart slow cooker. Place the potatoes in a single layer on top of the salt. Add more salt until the potatoes are completely covered. Cover and cook on high for 2 hours or until the potatoes are fork tender.

2. Crack the salt crust and remove the potatoes. Rub them with a towel to remove all of the salt before serving.

Kosher salt, as needed
4 medium-to-large russet potatoes

Per Serving

Calories	Fat	Sodium	Carbohydrates	Fiber	Protein
290	0g	25mg	64g	7g	8g

Dill Carrots

1. Place all ingredients in a 2-quart slow cooker. Stir. Cook on low 1½–2 hours or until the carrots are fork tender.

2. Stir before serving.

1 pound carrots, cut into coin-sized pieces

1 tablespoon minced fresh dill

½ teaspoon butter

3 tablespoons water

Per Serving

Calories	Fat	Sodium	Carbohydrates	Fiber	Protein
35	0g	40mg	8g	2g	1g

Rosemary-Thyme Green Beans

1. Place all ingredients in a 2-quart slow cooker. Stir to distribute the spices evenly.

2. Cook on low for 1½ hours or until the green beans are tender. Stir before serving.

1 pound green beans

1 tablespoon minced rosemary

1 teaspoon minced fresh thyme

2 tablespoons lemon juice

2 tablespoons water

Per Serving

Calories	Fat	Sodium	Carbohydrates	Fiber	Protein
40	0g	5mg	9g	4g	2g

Three Bean Salad

Three Bean Salad

1. Place the kidney beans, chickpeas, green beans, red peppers, red onions, fennel, and water in a 4-quart slow cooker. Cook on high for 2 hours or on low for 4 hours. Drain.

2. In a small bowl, whisk the salt, pepper, basil, lemon juice, mustard, vinegar, oil, garlic, and capers. Pour over the beans. Toss to coat.

15 ounces canned dark red kidney beans, drained and rinsed

15 ounces canned chickpeas, drained and rinsed

1 pound green beans

2 red bell peppers, chopped

½ cup thinly sliced red onion

½ cup thinly sliced fennel

½ cup water

¼ teaspoon salt

¼ teaspoon freshly ground black pepper

1 teaspoon minced fresh basil

2 tablespoons lemon juice

2 tablespoons Dijon mustard

2 tablespoons red wine vinegar

2 tablespoons olive oil

1 clove garlic, minced

1 teaspoon nonpareil capers

Per Serving

Calories	Fat	Sodium	Carbohydrates	Fiber	Protein
110	3g	350mg	18g	5g	5g

Stewed Tomatoes

Place all ingredients in a 2-quart slow cooker. Stir. Cook on low for up to 8 hours.

28 ounces canned whole tomatoes in purée, cut up

1 tablespoon minced onion

1 stalk celery, diced

½ teaspoon oregano

½ teaspoon thyme

Per Serving

Calories	Fat	Sodium	Carbohydrates	Fiber	Protein
25	0g	180mg	6g	1g	1g

Gingered Sweet Potatoes

1. Peel and quarter the sweet potatoes. Add them to a 4-quart slow cooker. Add the water, fresh ginger, and candied ginger. Stir.

2. Cook on high for 3–4 hours or until the potatoes are tender. Add the butter and mash. Serve immediately or turn them down to low to keep warm for up to 3 hours.

2½ pounds sweet potatoes

1 cup water

1 tablespoon grated fresh ginger

½ tablespoon minced uncrystallized candied ginger

½ tablespoon butter

Per Serving

Calories	Fat	Sodium	Carbohydrates	Fiber	Protein
100	0.5g	65mg	23g	3g	2g

Sweet and Sour Red Cabbage

1. Place all ingredients in a 4-quart slow cooker. Stir to distribute all ingredients evenly.

2. Cook on low for 4–6 hours or until the cabbage is very soft. Stir before serving.

½ head red cabbage, shredded

1 medium onion, shredded

1½ tablespoons dark brown sugar

1 teaspoon butter

¼ cup water

½ cup apple cider vinegar

1 tablespoon white wine vinegar

½ teaspoon freshly ground black pepper

¼ teaspoon salt

⅛ teaspoon ground cloves

½ teaspoon thyme

Per Serving

Calories	Fat	Sodium	Carbohydrates	Fiber	Protein
60	1g	135mg	13g	3g	2g

Mixed Summer Vegetables

1. Place the onions on the bottom of a 1½- or 2-quart slow cooker. Top with zucchini, yellow squash, thyme, lemon juice, salt, and pepper. Cook on low for 3½ hours.

2. Add the corn, okra, and butter, and stir. Cook on high for an additional 30 minutes.

1 medium onion, cut into ¼" slices

1½ cups sliced zucchini

1½ cups sliced yellow squash

1 tablespoon minced fresh thyme

¼ cup lemon juice

¼ teaspoon salt

¼ teaspoon black pepper

¾ cup fresh corn kernels

½ cup diced okra

1 teaspoon butter

Per Serving

Calories	Fat	Sodium	Carbohydrates	Fiber	Protein
80	1.5g	160mg	16g	3g	3g

Miso Eggplant

Place the water and miso in a 4-quart slow cooker. Stir to dissolve the miso. Add the eggplant and toss. Cook on high for 3 hours.

2 tablespoons water

¼ cup miso paste

1 (1-pound) eggplant, cubed

Per Serving

Calories	Fat	Sodium	Carbohydrates	Fiber	Protein
60	0g	540mg	12g	7g	4g

Stewed Okra

Place all ingredients in a 2-quart slow cooker and stir. Cook on low for 2–3 hours. Stir before serving.

Per Serving

Calories	Fat	Sodium	Carbohydrates	Fiber	Protein
40	0g	40mg	8g	3g	2g

2 large tomatoes, diced

1½ cups diced okra

1 small onion, diced

2 cloves garlic, minced

1 teaspoon hot sauce

Caramelized Onions

1. Peel and slice the onions into ¼" slices. Separate them into rings. Thinly slice the butter.

2. Place the onions in a 4-quart slow cooker. Scatter the butter slices over the top of the onions and drizzle with balsamic vinegar. At this point, the slow cooker may look full, but the onions will quickly reduce. Cover and cook on low for 10 hours.

3. If after 10 hours the onions are wet, turn the slow cooker up to high and cook, uncovered, for an additional 30 minutes or until the liquid evaporates.

4 pounds Vidalia or other sweet onions

3 tablespoons butter

1 tablespoon balsamic vinegar

Per 2 tablespoons

Calories	Fat	Sodium	Carbohydrates	Fiber	Protein
35	1g	0mg	6g	<1g	1g

Corn Bread

1. In a medium bowl, whisk together all ingredients except the cooking spray. Spray a 4-quart round slow cooker with the cooking spray.

2. Pour the batter into the slow cooker and cook on high for 2 hours. Slice the corn bread and lift out the slices.

1½ cups stone-ground cornmeal

¾ cup all-purpose flour

1 cup fat-free evaporated milk

1 tablespoon sugar

¼ teaspoon salt

1 cup fresh corn kernels

3½ tablespoons canola oil

2 eggs

Nonstick cooking spray, as needed

Per Serving

Calories	Fat	Sodium	Carbohydrates	Fiber	Protein
280	9g	130mg	43g	3g	8g

Corn on the Cob

Corn on the Cob

Place the corn in the bottom of an oval 4-quart slow cooker. Fill the insert with water until the water level is 1" below the top. Add salt. Cover and cook on low for 5 hours or on high for 2 hours. Garnish with parsley and serve hot.

6 ears corn, husks removed

Water, as needed

½ teaspoon salt

1 tablespoon minced fresh parsley

Per Serving

Calories	Fat	Sodium	Carbohydrates	Fiber	Protein
80	1g	210mg	17g	2g	3g

"Steamed" Artichokes

1. Cut the stems cut off of the artichokes and score the bottoms with a knife. Remove the outermost leaves.

2. Place the artichokes stem-side down in an oval 4-quart slow cooker. Pour the water into the bottom of the slow cooker. Add the lemons, lemon juice, and oregano.

3. Cook on low for 6 hours or until the leaves are tender.

4 large artichokes
1 cup water
1 lemon, cut into eighths
2 tablespoons lemon juice
1 teaspoon dried oregano

Per Serving

Calories	Fat	Sodium	Carbohydrates	Fiber	Protein
80	0g	150mg	19g	9g	5g

6

SAUCES AND SPREADS

Homemade Barbecue Sauce

Place all ingredients in a 1½- or 2-quart slow cooker. Whisk to combine. Cook on low for 2–3 hours. Whisk smooth. Refrigerate any leftover sauce in an airtight container for up to 3 weeks.

Per Serving

Calories	Fat	Sodium	Carbohydrates	Fiber	Protein
5	0g	65mg	1g	0g	0g

12 ounces tomato paste

2 cups distilled white vinegar

2 tablespoons dark brown sugar

1½ tablespoons mustard powder

1 tablespoon freshly ground black pepper

1½ tablespoons cayenne

1 teaspoon salt

1 tablespoon unsalted butter

Puttanesca Sauce

1. Pat the anchovies with a paper towel to remove any excess oil. Heat the olive oil in a large nonstick skillet and add the anchovies, garlic, and onions. Sauté until the anchovies mostly disappear into the onions, and the garlic and onions are soft.

2. Place the onions, anchovies, and garlic in a 4-quart slow cooker. Add the remaining ingredients. Stir to distribute the ingredients evenly. Cook on low for 10–12 hours. If the sauce looks very wet at the end of the cooking time, remove the lid and cook on high for 15–30 minutes before serving.

4 anchovies in oil

1 tablespoon olive oil

4 cloves garlic, minced

1 onion, diced

1 cup sliced black olives

28 ounces canned crushed tomatoes

15 ounces canned diced tomatoes

1 tablespoon red pepper flakes

2 tablespoons drained nonpareil capers

Per Serving

Calories	Fat	Sodium	Carbohydrates	Fiber	Protein
90	3g	580mg	16g	5g	4g

Rosemary-Mushroom Sauce

1. Melt the butter in a nonstick skillet. Add the onions and mushrooms and sauté until the onions are soft, about 5 minutes.

2. Place the onions and mushrooms in a 4-quart slow cooker. Add the rosemary and Chicken Stock. Stir. Cook on low for 6–8 hours or on high for 3.

1 teaspoon butter

1 large onion, thinly sliced

8 ounces sliced mushrooms

1 tablespoon crushed rosemary

3 cups Chicken Stock (Chapter 4)

Per Serving

Calories	Fat	Sodium	Carbohydrates	Fiber	Protein
100	3.5g	260mg	13g	2g	7g

Jalapeño-Tomatillo Sauce

1. Heat the oil in a nonstick pan. Sauté the garlic, onions, tomatillos, and jalapeños until softened.

2. Place the mixture in a 4-quart slow cooker. Add the water and stir. Cook on low for 8 hours.

1 teaspoon canola oil

2 cloves garlic, minced

1 onion, sliced

7 large-diced tomatillos

2 jalapeños, minced

½ cup water

Per Serving

Calories	Fat	Sodium	Carbohydrates	Fiber	Protein
50	2g	0mg	8g	2g	1g

Fruity Balsamic Barbecue Sauce

1. Place all ingredients in a 2-quart slow cooker. Stir. Cook on low for 6–8 hours.

2. Mash the sauce with a potato masher. Store in an airtight container for up to 2 weeks in the refrigerator.

¼ cup balsamic vinegar

2½ cups cubed mango

2 chipotle peppers in adobo, puréed

1 teaspoon dark brown sugar

Per Serving

Calories	Fat	Sodium	Carbohydrates	Fiber	Protein
20	0g	40mg	5g	0g	0g

Shrimp Fra Diavolo

1. Heat the oil in a nonstick skillet. Sauté the onions, garlic, and red pepper flakes until the onions are soft and translucent.

2. Add the onion mixture, tomatoes, parsley, and black pepper to a 4-quart slow cooker. Stir. Cook on low for 2–3 hours.

3. Add the shrimp. Stir. Cover and cook on high for 15 minutes or until the shrimp are fully cooked. Serve with spaghetti.

1 teaspoon olive oil

1 medium onion, diced

3 cloves garlic, minced

1 teaspoon red pepper flakes

15 ounces canned diced fire-roasted tomatoes

1 tablespoon minced fresh Italian parsley

½ teaspoon freshly ground black pepper

¾ pound medium shrimp, shelled

Per Serving

Calories	Fat	Sodium	Carbohydrates	Fiber	Protein
140	2.5g	170mg	11g	3g	19g

Shrimp Fra Diavolo

Artichoke Sauce

1. Heat the oil in a nonstick skillet. Sauté the artichokes, garlic, and onions until the onions are translucent and most of the liquid has evaporated. Put the mixture in a 4-quart slow cooker. Stir in the capers and crushed tomatoes.

2. Cook on high for 4 hours or on low for 8.

1 teaspoon olive oil

8 ounces frozen artichoke hearts, defrosted

3 cloves garlic, minced

1 medium onion, minced

2 tablespoons capote capers

28 ounces canned crushed tomatoes

Per Serving

Calories	Fat	Sodium	Carbohydrates	Fiber	Protein
120	2g	420mg	24g	7g	6g

Lemon Dill Sauce

Place all ingredients in a 2- or 4-quart slow cooker. Cook on high, uncovered, for 3 hours or until the sauce reduces by one-third.

2 cups Chicken Stock (Chapter 4)
½ cup lemon juice
½ cup minced fresh dill
¼ teaspoon white pepper

Per Serving

Calories	Fat	Sodium	Carbohydrates	Fiber	Protein
50	1.5g	170mg	7g	0g	3g

Raspberry Coulis

Place all ingredients in a 2-quart slow cooker. Mash gently with a potato masher. Cook on low, uncovered, for 4 hours. Stir before serving.

12 ounces fresh or frozen raspberries
1 teaspoon balsamic vinegar
2 tablespoons sugar

Per Serving

Calories	Fat	Sodium	Carbohydrates	Fiber	Protein
35	0g	0mg	8g	3g	1g

Pineapple-Mango Chutney

Pineapple-Mango Chutney

1. Put all ingredients in a 2- or 4-quart slow cooker. Stir. Cook on high for 3 hours or until soft.

2. Uncover and continue to cook on high for 1 hour.

Per Serving

Calories	Fat	Sodium	Carbohydrates	Fiber	Protein
130	0g	10mg	34g	2g	1g

3 cups cubed fresh pineapple

1½ cups cubed fresh mango

1 tablespoon grated fresh ginger

2 tablespoons minced onion

¼ cup balsamic vinegar

2 cloves garlic, minced

3 tablespoons lime juice

⅓ cup dark brown sugar

1 jalapeño, minced

Summer Berry Sauce

Place all ingredients in a 2-quart slow cooker. Lightly mash the berries with the back of a spoon. Cook on low for 2 hours, then uncover and cook on high for ½ hour.

1 cup raspberries

1 cup blackberries

1 cup golden raspberries

½ cup water

½ teaspoon sugar

Per Serving

Calories	Fat	Sodium	Carbohydrates	Fiber	Protein
10	0g	0mg	2g	1g	0g

Fennel and Caper Sauce

Place all ingredients except the parsley in an oval 4-quart slow cooker. Cook on low for 2 hours, then add the parsley. Cook on high an additional 15–30 minutes.

Per Serving

Calories	Fat	Sodium	Carbohydrates	Fiber	Protein
100	1g	390mg	21g	5g	4g

2 bulbs fennel with fronds, thinly sliced

2 tablespoons nonpareil capers

½ cup Chicken Stock (Chapter 4)

2 shallots, thinly sliced

2 cups diced fresh tomatoes

¼ teaspoon salt

½ teaspoon freshly ground black pepper

⅓ cup minced fresh parsley

Tomato and Chicken Sausage Sauce

1. Quickly brown the sausage slices on both sides in a non-stick skillet. Drain any grease. Add the sausages to a 4-quart slow cooker, along with the remaining ingredients. Stir.

2. Cook on low for 8 hours.

Per Serving

Calories	Fat	Sodium	Carbohydrates	Fiber	Protein
80	2g	320mg	14g	3g	4g

4 Italian chicken sausages, sliced

2 tablespoons tomato paste

28 ounces canned crushed tomatoes

3 cloves garlic, minced

1 onion, minced

3 tablespoons minced fresh basil

1 tablespoon minced fresh Italian parsley

¼ teaspoon crushed rosemary

¼ teaspoon freshly ground black pepper

Chicken Meatball Sun-Dried Tomato Sauce

1. Preheat the oven to 375°F. Line two baking sheets with parchment paper. In a large bowl, use your hands to mix the chicken, bread crumbs, egg, and minced garlic and shallot. Form into 1" balls. Place on the baking sheets and bake for 15 minutes or until cooked through.

2. Pour the crushed tomatoes into a 4-quart slow cooker. Add the sun-dried tomatoes, onions, and basil. Stir. Add the meatballs and stir to coat with sauce. Cook on low for 6 hours.

1 pound ground chicken

½ cup bread crumbs

1 egg

2 cloves garlic, minced

1 shallot, minced

28 ounces canned crushed tomatoes

½ cup julienne-cut dry (not oil-packed) sun-dried tomatoes

1 onion, minced

1 tablespoon minced fresh basil

Per Serving

Calories	Fat	Sodium	Carbohydrates	Fiber	Protein
220	8g	400mg	23g	4g	18g

Roasted Garlic Spread

½ tablespoon olive oil

4 heads garlic

1. Pour the oil onto the bottom of a 2-quart slow cooker. Place the garlic in a single layer on top.

2. Cook on low for 4–6 hours or until the garlic is very soft and golden. To serve, simply squeeze the garlic out of the skin.

Per 1 tablespoon

Calories	Fat	Sodium	Carbohydrates	Fiber	Protein
25	1g	0mg	4g	0g	1g

Roasted Garlic Spread

Cranberry Sauce

Place all ingredients in a 1½- or 2-quart slow cooker. Cook on high for 2½ hours. Stir before serving.

12 ounces fresh cranberries

½ cup freshly squeezed orange juice

½ cup water

½ teaspoon orange zest

½ teaspoon agave nectar

Per Serving

Calories	Fat	Sodium	Carbohydrates	Fiber	Protein
20	0g	0mg	5g	2g	0g

Blackberry Compote

Place all ingredients in a 2-quart slow cooker. Cook on low for 3 hours, remove the lid, and cook on high for 4 hours.

2 cups blackberries

¼ cup sugar

¼ cup water

Per Serving

Calories	Fat	Sodium	Carbohydrates	Fiber	Protein
50	0g	0mg	13g	2g	1g

Chipotle Tomato Sauce

Place all ingredients in a 4-quart slow cooker. Cook on low for 8–10 hours. Stir before serving.

Per Serving

Calories	Fat	Sodium	Carbohydrates	Fiber	Protein
70	0.5g	390mg	16g	5g	3g

3 cloves garlic, minced

1 onion, minced

28 ounces canned crushed tomatoes

14 ounces canned diced tomatoes

3 chipotle peppers in adobo, minced

1 teaspoon dried oregano

1 tablespoon minced fresh cilantro

½ teaspoon freshly ground black pepper

Pear Butter

1. Place all ingredients in a 4-quart slow cooker. Cook on low for 10–12 hours or until thick and most of the liquid has evaporated.
2. Allow to cool completely, then pour into the food processor and purée. Pour into clean glass jars. Refrigerate.

9 Bartlett pears, sliced
1 cup water or pear cider
¼ cup brown sugar
¼ cup sugar
¼ teaspoon ground ginger
¼ teaspoon cinnamon
¼ teaspoon mace

Per 2 tablespoons

Calories	Fat	Sodium	Carbohydrates	Fiber	Protein
15	0g	0mg	3g	0g	0g

Fig and Ginger Spread

1. Place all ingredients in a 2-quart slow cooker. Stir. Cook on low for 2–3 hours. Remove the lid and cook an additional 2–3 hours until the mixture is thickened.
2. Allow to cool completely, then pour into airtight containers and refrigerate up to 6 weeks.

2 pounds fresh figs
2 tablespoons minced fresh ginger
2 tablespoons lime juice
½ cup water
¾ cup sugar

Per Serving

Calories	Fat	Sodium	Carbohydrates	Fiber	Protein
50	0g	0mg	13g	1g	0g

POULTRY ENTRÉES

Mushroom Turkey Breast

1. Heat the butter in a nonstick skillet. Add the onions and mushrooms and sauté until the onions begin to soften. Add half of the onion and mushroom mixture to a 4-quart slow cooker. Add the turkey. Sprinkle with sage, salt, and pepper. Top with the remaining onion and mushroom mixture.

2. Add the water. Cook on high for 2–3 hours or on low for 6–8 hours.

1 teaspoon butter

1 medium onion, sliced

8 ounces sliced crimini mushrooms

1½ pounds turkey breast cutlets

1 teaspoon minced fresh sage

⅛ teaspoon salt

¼ teaspoon freshly ground black pepper

¼ cup water

Per Serving

Calories	Fat	Sodium	Carbohydrates	Fiber	Protein
150	1.5g	110mg	3g	<1g	29g

Sweet and Spicy Pulled Chicken

1. Place all ingredients in a round 2- or 4-quart slow cooker. Cook on low for 3½ hours, or for 1½ hours on low and then turn up to high for an additional hour.

2. When done, the meat should shred easily with a fork. Thoroughly shred the chicken. Toss to coat the chicken evenly with the sauce.

Per Serving

Calories	Fat	Sodium	Carbohydrates	Fiber	Protein
470	22g	440mg	12g	1g	52g

1¾ pounds boneless, skinless chicken thighs

¼ cup chili sauce

¼ cup balsamic vinegar

2 tablespoons ginger preserves

2 tablespoons pineapple juice

2 tablespoons lime juice

1 teaspoon cayenne

½ teaspoon ground chipotle

½ teaspoon hot paprika

1 jalapeño, minced

3 cloves garlic, minced

1 teaspoon yellow hot sauce

Tarragon Chicken

1. Place the chicken in a 4-quart slow cooker. Top with remaining ingredients. Cook on low for 7–8 hours.

2. Remove the chicken from the slow cooker. Peel off the skin and discard. Discard the tarragon and onions.

2 split chicken breasts

2 cups loosely packed fresh tarragon

1 onion, sliced

¼ teaspoon salt

¼ teaspoon freshly ground black pepper

Per Serving

Calories	Fat	Sodium	Carbohydrates	Fiber	Protein
100	1.5g	190mg	5g	0g	15g

Chicken Braised in Beer

1. Place all ingredients in a 4-quart slow cooker. Cook on low for 6 hours.

2. Remove the chicken breasts and discard the cooking liquid.

3 boneless, skinless chicken breasts

1 onion, quartered

6 ounces beer

1½ cups water

2 cloves garlic

Per Serving

Calories	Fat	Sodium	Carbohydrates	Fiber	Protein
80	0.5g	40mg	2g	0g	14g

Caribbean Chicken Curry

1. In a medium bowl, whisk together the curry powder, allspice, cloves, nutmeg, and ginger. Add the chicken and toss to coat each piece evenly.

2. Place the chicken in a nonstick skillet and quickly sauté until the chicken starts to brown. Add to a 4-quart slow cooker along with the remaining spice mixture.

3. Heat the oil in a nonstick skillet and sauté the onions, garlic, and jalapeños until fragrant. Add to the slow cooker.

4. Add the potatoes and coconut milk to the slow cooker. Stir. Cook on low for 7–8 hours.

1 tablespoon Madras curry powder

1 teaspoon allspice

½ teaspoon ground cloves

½ teaspoon nutmeg

1 teaspoon ground ginger

2 pounds boneless, skinless chicken thighs, cubed

1 teaspoon canola oil

1 onion, chopped

2 cloves garlic, chopped

2 jalapeños, chopped

½ pound red skin potatoes, cubed

⅓ cup light coconut milk

Per Serving

Calories	Fat	Sodium	Carbohydrates	Fiber	Protein
290	15g	105mg	7g	1g	30g

Orange Chicken

Orange Chicken

1. Whisk together the soy sauce, preserves, and juice in a small bowl.

2. Arrange the orange slices along the bottom of a 4-quart slow cooker. Top with the chicken breasts. Pour the sauce over the chicken. Cook on low for 3 hours or until the chicken is thoroughly cooked. Serve with rice.

Per Serving

Calories	Fat	Sodium	Carbohydrates	Fiber	Protein
170	2.5g	560mg	10g	1g	26g

2 tablespoons dark soy sauce

2 tablespoons spiced ginger preserves

½ cup freshly squeezed orange juice

1 large orange, peeled and sliced into ⅛"-thick slices

3 boneless, skinless chicken breasts (about ¾ pound)

Moroccan Chicken

1. Place all of the spices, chicken, water, garlic, onions, and ginger in a 4-quart slow cooker. Cook on low for 5 hours.

2. Stir in the chickpeas and apricots and cook on high for 40 minutes.

Per Serving

Calories	Fat	Sodium	Carbohydrates	Fiber	Protein
210	4.5g	340mg	30g	5g	13g

½ teaspoon coriander

½ teaspoon cinnamon

¼ teaspoon salt

1 teaspoon cumin

4 boneless, skinless chicken thighs, diced

½ cup water

4 cloves garlic, minced

1 onion, thinly sliced

1" knob peeled fresh ginger, minced

15 ounces canned chickpeas, drained and rinsed

4 ounces dried apricots, halved

Ginger Caramelized Chicken

1. Cut the chicken breasts into 1"-wide strips. Heat the oil in a nonstick skillet. Add the chicken, garlic, ginger, chiles, and shallot. Sauté until the shallots and garlic are fragrant.

2. Add the mixture to a 4-quart slow cooker. Add the remaining ingredients and stir. Cook on low for 4–5 hours.

Per Serving

Calories	Fat	Sodium	Carbohydrates	Fiber	Protein
270	5g	810mg	15g	0g	38g

1 pound boneless, skinless chicken breasts

1 teaspoon canola oil

2 cloves garlic, minced

2 tablespoons minced fresh ginger

2 Thai bird chiles, minced

1 shallot, minced

2 tablespoons fish sauce

1 tablespoon caramel syrup

¼ cup Chicken Stock (Chapter 4)

Mango Duck Breast

Place all ingredients in a 4-quart slow cooker. Cook on low for 4 hours.

Per Serving

Calories	Fat	Sodium	Carbohydrates	Fiber	Protein
150	4g	70mg	10g	1g	17g

2 boneless, skinless duck breasts

1 large mango, cubed

¼ cup duck stock or Chicken Stock (Chapter 4)

1 tablespoon ginger juice

1 tablespoon minced hot pepper

1 tablespoon minced shallot

Tuscan Chicken

Place all ingredients in a 4-quart slow cooker. Stir. Cook on low for 4 hours or until the chicken is fully cooked.

Per Serving

Calories	Fat	Sodium	Carbohydrates	Fiber	Protein
230	5g	170mg	7g	0g	37g

1 pound boneless, skinless chicken breast tenderloins

4 cloves garlic, minced

1 shallot, minced

2 tablespoons white wine vinegar

1 tablespoon lemon juice

1 tablespoon minced fresh rosemary

1 cup Chicken Stock (Chapter 4)

Chicken with Figs

1. Cube the chicken. Quickly sauté the chicken in a dry non-stick skillet until it starts to turn white. Drain off any excess grease.
2. Place the chicken and remaining ingredients in a 4-quart slow cooker. Stir. Cook on low for 6 hours. Stir before serving.

Per Serving

Calories	Fat	Sodium	Carbohydrates	Fiber	Protein
230	6g	180mg	22g	3g	24g

½ pound boneless, skinless chicken thighs

¾ pound boneless, skinless chicken breasts

¾ cup dried figs

1 sweet potato, peeled and diced

1 onion, chopped

3 cloves garlic, minced

2 teaspoons cumin

1 teaspoon coriander

½ teaspoon cayenne pepper

½ teaspoon ground ginger

½ teaspoon turmeric

½ teaspoon ground orange peel

½ teaspoon freshly ground black pepper

2¾ cups Chicken Stock (Chapter 4)

¼ cup orange juice

Thai Peanut Chicken

1. Place the chicken, broccoli, Chicken Stock, peanuts, soy sauce, chiles, garlic, and ginger in a 4-quart slow cooker. Stir.

2. Cook on low for 4–5 hours or until the chicken is thoroughly cooked. Stir in the green onions prior to serving.

Per Serving

Calories	Fat	Sodium	Carbohydrates	Fiber	Protein
210	7g	620mg	6g	2g	28g

1 pound boneless, skinless chicken breasts, cubed

2 cups broccoli florets

1 cup Chicken Stock (Chapter 4)

¼ cup coarsely chopped peanuts

3 tablespoons dark soy sauce

2 tablespoons minced Thai bird chiles

2 tablespoons minced garlic

2 tablespoons minced fresh ginger

¼ cup diced green onions

Peruvian Chicken with Aji Verde

1. Spread the cloves of garlic over the chicken pieces. Place in an oval 4-quart slow cooker. Pour the red wine vinegar, cumin, sugar, and soy sauce over the chicken. Cook on low for 5 hours or until the chicken is thoroughly cooked.

2. In a food processor, pulse together the jalapeños, cilantro, water, cheese, cider vinegar, and salt.

3. Remove the chicken from the slow cooker. Remove and discard the skin. Spread the sauce on each breast. Return to the slow cooker and cook on low for 15 minutes before serving.

5 cloves garlic, mashed

2 bone-in chicken breasts

2 tablespoons red wine vinegar

1 teaspoon cumin

1 teaspoon sugar

2 tablespoons dark soy sauce

2 jalapeños, chopped

½ cup fresh cilantro

⅓ cup water

⅓ cup crumbled Cotija cheese

1 teaspoon apple cider vinegar

¼ teaspoon salt

Per Serving

Calories	Fat	Sodium	Carbohydrates	Fiber	Protein
230	16g	800mg	4g	<1g	19g

Chicken Saltimbocca

1. Wrap each tenderloin in prosciutto and 2 sage leaves. Secure with a toothpick if necessary. Place them in a single layer in an oval 4-quart slow cooker.

2. Pour the Chicken Stock over the chicken. Sprinkle with the capers. Cook on low for 5 hours or until the chicken is fully cooked. Discard the cooking liquid prior to serving. Serve with roasted vegetables and pasta.

4 boneless, skinless chicken breast tenderloins

4 paper-thin slices prosciutto

¼ cup fresh sage

1½ cups Chicken Stock (Chapter 4)

3 tablespoons capote capers

¼ cup fresh sage

Per Serving

Calories	Fat	Sodium	Carbohydrates	Fiber	Protein
150	9g	620mg	9g	<1g	9g

Chicken Saltimbocca

Balsamic Chicken and Spinach

1. Place all ingredients except the spinach in a 4-quart slow cooker. Stir. Cook on low for 6 hours.

2. Stir in the baby spinach and continue to cook until it starts to wilt, about 15 minutes. Stir before serving.

Per Serving

Calories	Fat	Sodium	Carbohydrates	Fiber	Protein
180	3g	125mg	10g	2g	28g

¾ pound boneless, skinless chicken breasts, cut into strips

¼ cup balsamic vinegar

4 cloves garlic, minced

1 tablespoon minced fresh oregano

1 tablespoon minced fresh Italian parsley

½ teaspoon freshly ground black pepper

5 ounces baby spinach

Poached Chicken

1. Place the chicken in an oval 6-quart slow cooker. Arrange the vegetables around the chicken. Add the water. Cook on low for 7–8 hours.

2. Remove the chicken skin before eating.

4–5 pounds whole chicken or chicken parts

1 carrot

1 stalk celery

1 onion, quartered

1 cup water

Per Serving

Calories	Fat	Sodium	Carbohydrates	Fiber	Protein
330	8g	220mg	3g	<1g	58g

Slow-Roasted Chicken with Potatoes, Parsnips, and Onions

SERVES 6

1. Cover the bottom of a 6- or 7-quart oval slow cooker with half of the onions.

2. Place the chicken, breast-side up, on top of the onions.

3. Cover the chicken with the remaining onions.

4. Arrange the potatoes and parsnips around the chicken. Add salt and black pepper

5. Cover and cook on low for 8 hours or until the chicken has an internal temperature of 165°F as measured using a food thermometer. Discard the chicken skin before serving.

4 medium onions, sliced

1 (6-pound) roasting chicken

6 large red skin potatoes, halved

4 parsnips, diced

1 teaspoon salt

1 teaspoon black pepper

Per Serving

Calories	Fat	Sodium	Carbohydrates	Fiber	Protein
730	10g	540mg	86g	11g	71g

Goan Chicken Curry

1. In a large nonstick skillet, heat the oil. Sauté the onions and garlic for 3 minutes.
2. Place all ingredients in a 6-quart slow cooker. Stir. Cover and cook on low for 6–8 hours. Stir before serving.

Per Serving

Calories	Fat	Sodium	Carbohydrates	Fiber	Protein
480	33g	230mg	11g	6g	37g

1 teaspoon canola oil

2 medium onions, diced

4 cloves garlic, minced

3 pounds boneless, skinless chicken thighs, cubed

1 tablespoon minced fresh ginger

2 cups toasted unsweetened shredded coconut

1 teaspoon cinnamon

¼ teaspoon nutmeg

½ teaspoon ground cloves

½ teaspoon salt

1 teaspoon cumin seeds

1 teaspoon black mustard seeds

2 tablespoons red pepper flakes

1½ cups water

Thyme-Roasted Turkey Breast

1. Arrange the onion slices in a thin layer on the bottom of a 6- or 7-quart slow cooker.

2. Make a small slit in the skin of the turkey and spread the thyme between the skin and meat. Smooth the skin back onto the turkey.

3. In a small bowl, stir the pepper, salt, parsley, celery flakes, and mustard seeds. Rub the spice mixture into the skin of the turkey.

4. Place the turkey in the slow cooker on top of the onion layer. Cook on low for 8 hours. Remove the turkey skin and onions and discard them before serving the turkey.

2 onions, thinly sliced

1 (6- to 7-pound) turkey breast or turkey half

½ cup minced fresh thyme

½ tablespoon freshly ground black pepper

½ tablespoon salt

½ tablespoon dried parsley

½ tablespoon celery flakes

½ tablespoon mustard seeds

Per Serving

Calories	Fat	Sodium	Carbohydrates	Fiber	Protein
450	19g	520mg	4g	1g	60g

Wild Rice–Stuffed Turkey Breast Cutlets

1. Place the onions and mushrooms on the bottom of a 4-quart slow cooker.

2. Divide the wild rice into four portions. Place a single portion in the center of each cutlet. Roll, rice-side in, and secure with a toothpick or kitchen twine. Place on top of the onions and mushrooms. Pour the stock over top.

3. Cook on low for 4 hours.

1 onion, sliced

4 ounces button mushrooms, minced

1 cup cooked wild rice

4 turkey breast cutlets (about 1 pound)

½ cup Chicken Stock (Chapter 4) or Spicy Smoked Turkey Stock (Chapter 4)

Per Serving

Calories	Fat	Sodium	Carbohydrates	Fiber	Protein
190	1g	150mg	12g	1g	31g

Filipino Chicken Adobo

Filipino Chicken Adobo

Place all ingredients in a 2-quart slow cooker. Cook on low for 6–8 hours. Discard the bay leaves before serving.

Per Serving

Calories	Fat	Sodium	Carbohydrates	Fiber	Protein
150	6g	2,060mg	7g	<1g	18g

2 boneless, skinless chicken thighs

¼ cup water

¼ cup cane vinegar

¼ cup dark soy sauce

1 teaspoon whole black peppercorns

5 cloves garlic, halved

2 bay leaves

Ginger-Glazed Cornish Game Hen

Place the Cornish game hen in a 2-quart slow cooker. In a small bowl, whisk the ginger and lime juice. Pour over the hen. Cook on low for 6–7 hours. Discard the skin before serving.

1 (4-pound) Cornish game hen
2 tablespoons ground ginger
2 tablespoons fresh lime juice

Per Serving

Calories	Fat	Sodium	Carbohydrates	Fiber	Protein
140	3.5g	55mg	5g	<1g	21g

Chicken Fricassee

1. Place the cabbage, carrots, celery, and onions on the bottom of an oval 4-quart slow cooker.

2. Place the chicken skin-side up on top of the vegetables. Pour the Chicken Stock over the chicken and sprinkle it evenly with the spices. Pat the spices onto the chicken skin.

3. Cook on low for 6 hours or until the chicken is cooked through. Remove the chicken skin prior to serving.

2 cups sliced red cabbage

2 carrots, cut into coin-sized pieces

2 stalks celery, diced

1 onion, sliced

3 bone-in chicken breasts

¾ cup Chicken Stock (Chapter 4)

2 teaspoons paprika

2 teaspoons thyme

2 teaspoons dried parsley

Per Serving

Calories	Fat	Sodium	Carbohydrates	Fiber	Protein
170	7g	130mg	9g	2g	17g

8

PORK ENTRÉES

Pork with Caramelized Onions, Roasted Potatoes, and Apples

1. Trim extra fat from the roast. Quickly sear it on all sides in a hot nonstick pan.

2. Place the roast in a 4-quart oval slow cooker. Top with the Caramelized Onions, potatoes, and apples. Add the water and vinegar, then sprinkle with the spices.

3. Cover and cook on low for 8 hours or until the pork is tender and falling apart.

1 (5-pound) boneless pork roast

1 cup Caramelized Onions (Chapter 5)

1 pound baby red skin potatoes

2 apples, cored and sliced

¼ cup water

¼ cup balsamic vinegar

1 teaspoon paprika

¼ teaspoon freshly ground black pepper

¼ teaspoon cinnamon

⅛ teaspoon salt

Per Serving

Calories	Fat	Sodium	Carbohydrates	Fiber	Protein
540	21g	180mg	19g	2g	64g

Smoky Mango Pulled Pork

SERVES 6

1. Place all ingredients in a 4-quart slow cooker. Cook on low for 8–9 hours or on high for 6 hours, or until the meat is easily shredded with a fork

2. Remove the roast from the slow cooker. Use two forks to shred the pork; set it aside. Mash any solid bits of the sauce in the slow cooker with a potato masher. Return the pork to the slow cooker, and toss to coat the meat evenly.

2½ pounds boneless pork roast, excess fat trimmed

1 mango, cubed

¼ cup chili sauce

¼ cup balsamic vinegar

1 tablespoon yellow hot sauce

1 teaspoon cayenne

1 teaspoon freshly ground black pepper

1 large onion, thinly sliced

1 teaspoon liquid smoke

3 cloves garlic, minced

1 teaspoon hot Mexican chili powder

1 habanero pepper, minced

2 tablespoons lime juice

Per Serving

Calories	Fat	Sodium	Carbohydrates	Fiber	Protein
440	17g	320mg	16g	1g	53g

Georgia-Style Pulled Pork Sandwiches

1. Place all ingredients in a 4-quart slow cooker. Cook on low for 8 hours or until the meat is easily shredded with a fork.

2. Remove the pork from the slow cooker to a plate. Shred the meat with a fork. Mash the remaining sauce and solids in the slow cooker with a potato masher until fairly smooth. Add the pork back to the slow cooker and toss to coat in the sauce. Serve on a bun with coleslaw.

3½ pounds boneless pork roast

1 cup Homemade Barbecue Sauce (Chapter 6)

1 large onion, diced

2 cloves garlic, minced

1 tablespoon hickory liquid smoke

1 jalapeño, sliced

Per Serving

Calories	Fat	Sodium	Carbohydrates	Fiber	Protein
410	18g	140mg	2g	0g	55g

Georgia-Style Pulled Pork Sandwiches

Chinese-Style Boneless Ribs

1. Heat the oil in a large skillet. Cook the pork for 1 minute on each side. Place in a 4-quart slow cooker. Pour the remaining ingredients over the meat. Cover and cook on low for 8 hours.

2. If the sauce is very thin, pour into a saucepan and cook until it reduces. Drizzle the sauce on the ribs and serve.

1 teaspoon canola oil

2 pounds boneless pork ribs

2 cloves garlic, minced

1 tablespoon red pepper flakes

1 small onion, minced

1 tablespoon five-spice powder

1 tablespoon black vinegar

¼ cup dark soy sauce

2 tablespoons lime juice

1 teaspoon sesame oil

Per Serving

Calories	Fat	Sodium	Carbohydrates	Fiber	Protein
530	26g	115mg	7g	<1g	64g

Pork Roast with Cranberry Sauce

1. Place the onion slices on the bottom of a 4-quart slow cooker. Top with the pork, then the dried cranberries, and finally the Cranberry Sauce to cover the whole roast.

2. Cover and cook on low for 8 hours. Remove the pork and slice it. Discard the cooking liquids.

1 medium onion, thinly sliced

1 (1¼-pound) pork loin

2 tablespoons sweetened dried cranberries

1 cup Cranberry Sauce (Chapter 6)

Per Serving

Calories	Fat	Sodium	Carbohydrates	Fiber	Protein
350	19g	105mg	7g	1g	36g

Tomato-Braised Pork

1. Place the tomatoes, tomato paste, basil, pepper, and marjoram in a 4-quart slow cooker. Stir to create a uniform sauce. Add the pork.

2. Cook on low for 7–8 hours or until the pork easily falls apart when poked with a fork.

28 ounces canned crushed tomatoes

3 tablespoons tomato paste

1 cup loosely packed fresh basil

½ teaspoon freshly ground black pepper

½ teaspoon marjoram

1 (1¼-pound) boneless pork roast

Per Serving

Calories	Fat	Sodium	Carbohydrates	Fiber	Protein
360	13g	450mg	17g	5g	43g

Boneless Pork Ribs

Boneless Pork Ribs

1. Rub both sides of the pork with the chipotle, salt, and pepper. Place in an oval 4-quart slow cooker.

2. In a small bowl, whisk together the remaining ingredients until smooth.

3. Pour the sauce over the ribs. Cook on low for 6–8 hours.

1¼ pounds boneless pork ribs

2 teaspoons ground chipotle

¼ teaspoon salt

1 teaspoon freshly ground black pepper

1 tablespoon ginger juice

2 tablespoons blackberry jam

½ cup chili sauce

½ tablespoon hickory liquid smoke

½ teaspoon garlic powder

½ teaspoon onion powder

2 tablespoons balsamic vinegar

1 teaspoon Worcestershire sauce

Per Serving

Calories	Fat	Sodium	Carbohydrates	Fiber	Protein
360	15g	600mg	13g	<1g	40g

Chinese Hot Pot

1. Place the ginger, Chicken Stock, water, onions, shiitake mushrooms, and garlic in a 4-quart slow cooker. Cook on low for 7–8 hours.

2. Add the pork, bok choy, enoki mushrooms, and noodles. Cook on high for 15–30 minutes.

Per Serving

Calories	Fat	Sodium	Carbohydrates	Fiber	Protein
470	11g	810mg	54g	8g	43g

1" knob peeled fresh ginger, sliced

1 quart Chicken Stock (Chapter 4)

2½ cups water

2 green onions, diced

¼ pound fresh shiitake mushrooms, sliced

3 cloves garlic

¾ pound very thinly sliced pork

3 heads baby bok choy, chopped

4 ounces enoki mushrooms

4 ounces cellophane noodles

Caribbean Pulled Pork

1. Place all ingredients in a 4-quart slow cooker. Cook on low for 8–10 hours or until the pork is easily shredded with a fork.

2. Remove the pork from the slow cooker. Place it on a plate and shred it with a fork. Mash the mixture in the slow cooker with a potato masher. Return the pork to the slow cooker and toss to coat.

Per Serving

Calories	Fat	Sodium	Carbohydrates	Fiber	Protein
340	12g	220mg	7g	<1g	46g

2 pounds pork loin

¼ cup chili sauce

1 Scotch bonnet pepper, minced

¼ cup red wine vinegar

½ teaspoon freshly ground black pepper

1 tablespoon ginger preserves

2 tablespoons orange juice

1 tablespoon lime juice

½ teaspoon allspice

½ teaspoon ground cloves

½ teaspoon cayenne pepper

½ teaspoon oregano

½ teaspoon cumin

½ teaspoon thyme

1 teaspoon hickory liquid smoke

1 onion, chopped

2 cloves garlic

Sour Cherry–Glazed Pork

1. In a small bowl, whisk the preserves, sour cherries, water, pepper, salt, and nutmeg.

2. Place the pork loin in a 4-quart slow cooker. Pour the glaze over the pork. Cook on low for 8 hours.

Per Serving

Calories	Fat	Sodium	Carbohydrates	Fiber	Protein
290	15g	210mg	7g	0g	30g

3 tablespoons ginger preserves

¼ cup dried sour cherries

⅔ cup water

¼ teaspoon freshly ground black pepper

¼ teaspoon salt

⅛ teaspoon nutmeg

1 (1¼-pound) pork loin

Glazed Lean Pork Shoulder

Place the pork shoulder in a 4-quart slow cooker. Top with the remaining ingredients. Cook on low for 8 hours. Remove the lid and cook on high for 30 minutes or until the sauce thickens.

Per Serving

Calories	Fat	Sodium	Carbohydrates	Fiber	Protein
280	11g	140mg	11g	2g	34g

1 (3-pound) bone-in pork shoulder, excess fat removed

3 apples, thinly sliced

¼ cup apple cider

1 tablespoon brown sugar

1 teaspoon allspice

½ teaspoon cinnamon

¼ teaspoon nutmeg

Chinese-Style Braised Pork

1. Heat a large nonstick skillet. Cook the pork for 1 minute on each side.

2. Place the pork in a 4-quart slow cooker. Pour the remaining ingredients over the meat. Cover and cook on low for 8 hours.

Per Serving

Calories	Fat	Sodium	Carbohydrates	Fiber	Protein
340	14g	850mg	5g	1g	47g

1 (1⅓-pound) pork loin

2 cloves garlic, minced

1 tablespoon red pepper flakes

1 small onion, minced

1 teaspoon ground ginger

1 teaspoon ground garlic

½ teaspoon cinnamon

½ teaspoon ground star anise

1 tablespoon rice vinegar

3 tablespoons dark soy sauce

1 teaspoon sesame oil

Jamaican Ham

1. Use toothpicks to attach half the pineapple chunks to the ham. Place it in a 4-quart slow cooker.

2. Pour the remaining pineapple chunks, juice, and spices over the ham. Cook on low for 6–8 hours.

3. Remove the ham from the slow cooker. Remove the toothpicks, placing the pineapple chunks back in the slow cooker. Stir the contents of the slow cooker.

4. Slice the ham and return it to the slow cooker. Toss with the juices prior to serving.

20 ounces canned pineapple chunks in juice

1 (1½-pound) boneless smoked ham quarter

1 tablespoon ground cloves

1 teaspoon allspice

1 teaspoon ground ginger

Per Serving

Calories	Fat	Sodium	Carbohydrates	Fiber	Protein
300	4.5g	1,550mg	34g	2g	31g

Slow-Cooked Char Siu
(Chinese Barbecue Pork)

Slow-Cooked Char Siu (Chinese Barbecue Pork)

1. Slice the pork into 3"-wide strips. Place the pork in a resealable plastic bag. Add the remaining ingredients. Refrigerate overnight.

2. Pour the pork and marinade into a 4-quart slow cooker. Cook on low for 8 hours.

Per Serving

Calories	Fat	Sodium	Carbohydrates	Fiber	Protein
330	14g	890mg	13g	<1g	34g

1½ pounds boneless pork rib, trimmed of excess fat

¼ cup dark soy sauce

¼ cup hoisin sauce

3 tablespoons Chinese rice wine

2 tablespoons golden syrup

1 tablespoon sesame seed paste or tahini

1 tablespoon lime zest

1 teaspoon grated fresh ginger

1 teaspoon minced garlic

1 teaspoon sesame oil

½ teaspoon five-spice powder

2 tablespoons lime juice

Blackberry Pulled Pork

1. Place all ingredients in a 6-quart slow cooker. Cook on low for 8–9 hours or on high for 6 hours, or until the meat is easily shredded with a fork.

2. Remove the pork from the slow cooker. Shred with a fork and set aside. Mash any solid bits of the sauce in the slow cooker with a potato masher. Return the pork to the slow cooker, and toss to coat the pork evenly with the sauce.

Per Serving

Calories	Fat	Sodium	Carbohydrates	Fiber	Protein
510	19g	510mg	13g	2g	68g

6 pounds boneless pork roast, excess fat removed

2 cups fresh blackberries

½ cup chili sauce

½ cup balsamic vinegar

¼ teaspoon lime juice

1 tablespoon ginger preserves

2 teaspoons mesquite liquid smoke

2 teaspoons freshly ground black pepper

1 teaspoon cayenne

1 teaspoon chili powder

1 teaspoon hot paprika

2 large onions, diced

5 cloves garlic, minced

¼ teaspoon salt

Pork Tenderloin with Fennel

Place the pork in an oval 6- or 7-quart slow cooker. Top with remaining ingredients. Cook on low for 8 hours.

Per Serving

Calories	Fat	Sodium	Carbohydrates	Fiber	Protein
250	7g	260mg	7g	3g	39g

1 (4-pound) pork tenderloin, excess fat removed

4 bulbs fennel, cubed

1½ cups Caramelized Onions (Chapter 5)

1 teaspoon freshly ground black pepper

½ teaspoon salt

Sticky Spicy Spare Ribs

1. Place the ribs on a broiler-safe platter. Broil on high until much of the fat has been rendered. Place in a 6- or 7-quart slow cooker.

2. In a small bowl, whisk the brown sugar, chili sauce, rice vinegar, garlic-chili sauce, and shallots. Pour over the ribs. Cook on low for 8 hours.

3. Remove spare ribs from the slow cooker. Place them on a baking sheet in a cold oven to keep warm. Transfer sauce to a small bowl. Drain off fat. Pour over the ribs before serving.

4 pounds lean pork spare ribs

2 tablespoons dark brown sugar

½ cup chili sauce

¼ cup rice vinegar

¼ cup garlic-chili sauce

1 shallot, minced

Per Serving

Calories	Fat	Sodium	Carbohydrates	Fiber	Protein
410	19g	870mg	13	0g	44g

Pineapple Pork Chops

1. Place the onion slices on the bottom of a 1½- or 2-quart slow cooker. Top with a pineapple slice. Center 1 pork chop over the pineapple slice. Top with a second pineapple slice. Center the second pork chop over the pineapple. Top with the last pineapple slice.

2. Add the soy sauce, ginger, and chiles. Cook on low for 8–10 hours.

1 small onion, sliced

3 (¼"-thick) fresh pineapple slices

½ pound thick-cut boneless pork chops

2 tablespoons dark soy sauce

1 teaspoon grated fresh ginger

3 Thai bird chiles, minced

Per Serving

Calories	Fat	Sodium	Carbohydrates	Fiber	Protein
300	10g	1,080mg	17g	2g	37g

Rhubarb Pulled Pork

SERVES 2

1. Quickly sear the pork on all sides in a nonstick skillet. Place in a 2-quart slow cooker. Add remaining ingredients. Cook on high for 5 hours.

2. Remove the pork from the slow cooker. Shred with a fork. Mash the rhubarb in the slow cooker with a potato masher until smooth. Add the pork back into the slow cooker and stir to distribute the sauce evenly.

1 (½-pound) pork loin

½ cup chopped rhubarb

1 small onion, diced

1 tablespoon ginger preserves

1 tablespoon chili sauce

Per Serving

Calories	Fat	Sodium	Carbohydrates	Fiber	Protein
260	10g	310mg	8g	1g	34g

Quinoa with Chorizo

SERVES 2

Sauté the chorizo and onions in a small nonstick saucepan until the onions are soft. Drain off any excess fat. Add to a 1½- or 2-quart slow cooker along with the quinoa and water. Cover and cook on low for 2 hours. Stir before serving.

¼ cup sliced lean Spanish-style chorizo

¼ cup sliced onions

½ cup quinoa, rinsed

1 cup water

Per Serving

Calories	Fat	Sodium	Carbohydrates	Fiber	Protein
300	14g	380mg	31g	3g	13g

9

BEEF AND LAMB ENTRÉES

Lean Roast with Fennel and Rutabaga

1. Peel and cube the rutabagas. Cut any excess fat off the roast. Sprinkle the salt and pepper on all sides of the roast.

2. Heat a nonstick skillet for 30 seconds. Place the roast in the pan. Quickly sear each side of the roast, approximately 5 seconds per side.

3. Place the roast in a 4-quart slow cooker. Cover it with the onions, rutabagas, and fennel.

4. Cook on low for 6 hours or until desired doneness.

1 pound rutabagas

1 (2-pound) boneless bottom round roast

½ teaspoon salt

½ teaspoon freshly ground black pepper

1 Vidalia or other sweet onion, sliced

2 bulbs fennel, sliced

Per Serving

Calories	Fat	Sodium	Carbohydrates	Fiber	Protein
450	18g	520mg	21g	7g	51g

Better-Than-Takeout Mongolian Beef

1. Place all ingredients in a 4-quart oval slow cooker. Cover and cook for 5 hours on low or until the meat is thoroughly cooked through and tender.

2. Remove the roast to a cutting board. Slice thinly and return it to the slow cooker. Cook on high for an additional 20 minutes. Stir the meat and the sauce before serving.

Per Serving

Calories	Fat	Sodium	Carbohydrates	Fiber	Protein
490	27g	930mg	10g	<1g	49g

1 (3-pound) lean beef bottom roast, extra fat removed

3 cloves garlic, grated

1" knob peeled fresh ginger, grated

1 medium onion, thinly sliced

½ cup water

½ cup low-sodium soy sauce

2 tablespoons black vinegar

2 tablespoons hoisin sauce

1 tablespoon five-spice powder

1 tablespoon cornstarch

1 teaspoon red pepper flakes

1 teaspoon sesame oil

9: BEEF AND LAMB ENTRÉES   187

Rouladen

Rouladen

1. Pour the wine and water into the bottom of an oval 4-quart slow cooker.

2. Place the steaks horizontally on a platter. Spread ½ tablespoon mustard on each steak and sprinkle each with one-quarter of the bacon crumbles, if using. Place one of the pickle spears on one end of each steak. Starting from this end, roll each steak toward the other end, so it looks like a spiral. Heat a skillet and place the steak rolls in the skillet seam-side down. Cook for 1 minute, then use tongs to flip the steak rolls carefully and cook the other side for 1 minute.

3. Place steak rolls in a single layer in the water-wine mixture. Cook on low for 1 hour. Remove the rolls, discarding the cooking liquid.

¼ cup red wine

1 cup water

4 very thin round steaks (about ¾ pound total)

2 tablespoons grainy German-style mustard

1 tablespoon lean bacon crumbles (optional)

4 dill pickle spears

Per Serving

Calories	Fat	Sodium	Carbohydrates	Fiber	Protein
180	7g	970mg	7g	<1g	20g

Stuffed Cabbage

SERVES 4

1. Bring a large pot of water to boil. Meanwhile, using a knife, make 4 or 5 cuts around the core of the cabbage and remove the core. Discard the core and 2 layers of the outer leaves. Peel off 6–8 large whole leaves. Place the leaves in a steamer basket and allow them to steam over the boiling water for 7 minutes. Allow the leaves to cool enough to handle. Dice the remaining cabbage to equal ½ cup.

2. In a nonstick skillet, melt the butter. Add the sliced onions and diced cabbage, and sauté until the onions are soft. Add the tomatoes. Break up the tomatoes into small chunks using the back of a spoon. Simmer until the sauce has reduced, about 10–15 minutes. Ladle about one-third of the sauce over the bottom of a 4-quart oval slow cooker.

3. Place the minced onions, egg, rice, spices, and beef in a medium-sized bowl. Stir to distribute all ingredients evenly.

4. Place a cabbage leaf with the open side up and the stem part facing you on a clean work area. Add about ¼ cup filling to the leaf toward the stem. Fold the sides together, and then pull the top down and over the filling to form a packet. It should look like a burrito. Repeat until all the filling is gone.

5. Arrange the cabbage rolls, seam-side down, in a single layer in the slow cooker. Ladle about half of the remaining sauce over the rolls and repeat with a second layer. Ladle the remaining sauce over the rolls. Cover and cook on low for up to 10 hours.

Water, as needed

1 large head cabbage

1 teaspoon butter

½ cup sliced onions

28 ounces canned whole tomatoes in purée

½ cup minced onions

1 egg

1½ cups cooked long-grain rice

½ tablespoon garlic powder

½ tablespoon paprika

1 pound 94% lean ground beef

Per Serving

Calories	Fat	Sodium	Carbohydrates	Fiber	Protein
370	8g	150mg	47g	10g	33g

Cottage Pie with Carrots, Parsnips, and Celery

1. Sauté the onions, garlic, carrots, parsnips, celery, and beef in a large nonstick skillet until the ground beef is browned. Drain off any excess fat and discard it. Place the mixture in a round 4-quart slow cooker. Add the stock, paprika, rosemary, Worcestershire sauce, savory, salt, and pepper. Stir.

2. Cook on low for 6–8 hours. If the meat mixture still looks very wet, create a slurry by mixing together 1 tablespoon cornstarch and 1 tablespoon water. Stir this into the meat mixture.

3. In a medium bowl, mash the parsley and potatoes using a potato masher. Spread on top of the ground beef mixture in the slow cooker. Cover and cook on high for 30–60 minutes or until the potatoes are warmed through.

1 large onion, diced

3 cloves garlic, minced

1 carrot, diced

1 parsnip, diced

1 stalk celery, diced

1 pound 94% lean ground beef

1½ cups beef stock

½ teaspoon hot paprika

½ teaspoon crushed rosemary

1 tablespoon Worcestershire sauce

½ teaspoon dried savory

⅛ teaspoon salt

¼ teaspoon freshly ground black pepper

1 tablespoon cornstarch and 1 tablespoon water, mixed (if necessary)

¼ cup minced fresh parsley

2¾ cups plain mashed potatoes

Per Serving

Calories	Fat	Sodium	Carbohydrates	Fiber	Protein
240	6g	420mg	26g	2g	21g

Slimmed-Down Moussaka

1. Slice the eggplants crosswise into ¼"-thick slices. Place in a colander and lightly salt the eggplant. Allow to drain for 15 minutes. Meanwhile, preheat the oven to 375°F. Rinse off the eggplant slices and pat them dry. Arrange the slices in a single layer on two parchment paper–lined baking sheets. Bake for 15 minutes.

2. While prepping the eggplant, heat the oil in a nonstick skillet. Sauté the onions and garlic for 1 minute, then add the tomatoes, tomato paste, cinnamon, oregano, parsley, and ground beef. Break up the tomatoes into small chunks using the back of a spoon. Simmer, stirring occasionally, until the meat is browned and most of the liquid evaporates.

3. Ladle half of the sauce onto the bottom of a 4- or 6-quart oval slow cooker. Top with a single layer of eggplant, taking care to leave no gaps between slices. Top with remaining sauce. Top with another layer of eggplant. Cover with the lid and cook on high for 2½–3 hours or on low for up to 6 hours.

4. In a small saucepan, whisk together the evaporated milk, butter, egg, and flour. Bring to a boil and then reduce the heat. Whisk until smooth.

5. Pour the sauce over the eggplant and cook for an additional 1–1½ hours on high.

2 (1-pound) eggplants, peeled

Salt, as needed

1 teaspoon olive oil

1 large onion, diced

2 cloves garlic, minced

20 ounces canned whole tomatoes in purée

1 tablespoon tomato paste

½ teaspoon cinnamon

1 tablespoon minced oregano

1 tablespoon minced flat-leaf parsley

1 pound 94% lean ground beef

1 cup fat-free evaporated milk

1 tablespoon butter

1 egg

2 tablespoons flour

Per Serving

Calories	Fat	Sodium	Carbohydrates	Fiber	Protein
250	8g	150mg	24g	7g	24g

Corned Beef and Cabbage

1. Trim excess fat off the brisket. Cut into 1" cubes.
2. Add the brisket and all of the remaining ingredients to a 4-quart slow cooker. Cook on low for 10 hours.

Per Serving

Calories	Fat	Sodium	Carbohydrates	Fiber	Protein
270	13g	95mg	24g	7g	14g

1 (¾-pound) corned beef brisket

1 head green cabbage, cut into wedges

2 carrots, sliced

2 parsnips, sliced

2 cups water

1 onion, sliced

1 teaspoon yellow mustard seeds

Beef and Guinness Stew

1. Heat the oil in a large skillet. Sauté the onions, parsnips, carrots, celery, garlic, potatoes, rosemary, and beef until the ingredients begin to soften and brown. Drain any excess fat.

2. Add to a 4-quart slow cooker. Sprinkle with brown sugar, salt, pepper, and cocoa. Pour in the water and Guinness. Stir. Cook on low for 8–9 hours.

3. Add the frozen peas. Cover and cook on high for an additional ½ hour. Stir before serving and garnish with parsley.

Per Serving

Calories	Fat	Sodium	Carbohydrates	Fiber	Protein
230	5g	170mg	25g	4g	27g

2 teaspoons canola oil

1 large onion, diced

2 parsnips, sliced

2 carrots, sliced

2 stalks celery, diced

3 cloves garlic, minced

2 russet potatoes, chunked or sliced

2 tablespoons minced fresh rosemary

2 pounds lean top round roast, cut into 1" cubes

1 tablespoon dark brown sugar

¼ teaspoon salt

½ teaspoon freshly ground black pepper

1 tablespoon baking cocoa

1 cup water

½ cup Guinness Extra Stout

½ cup frozen peas

1 tablespoon minced fresh parsley

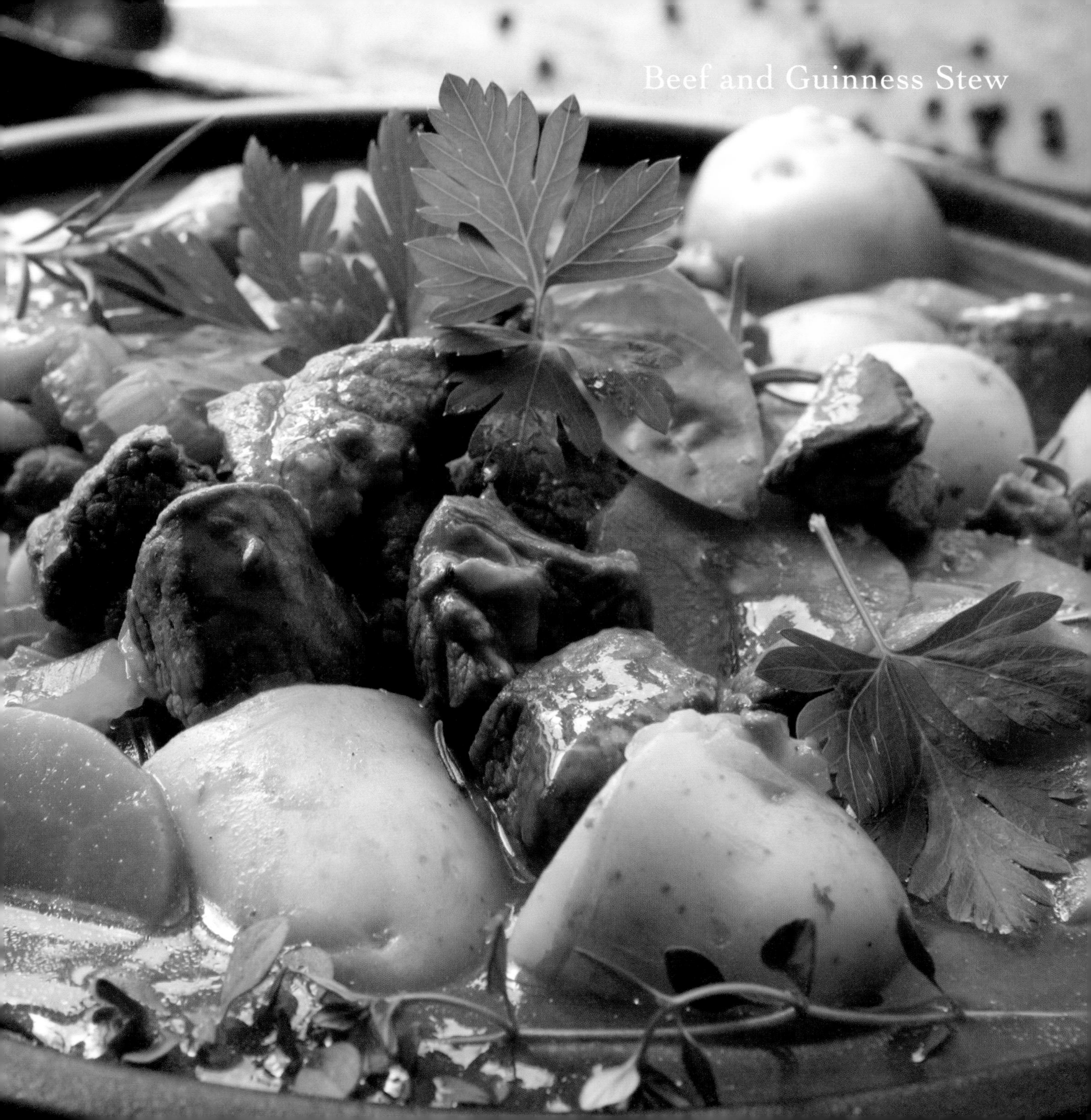
Beef and Guinness Stew

Ropa Vieja

1. Place the roast, pepper, onions, carrots, tomatoes, garlic, oregano, and cumin in a 2-quart slow cooker. Cook on high for 7 hours. Add the olives and continue to cook for 20 minutes.

2. Shred the meat with a fork, then stir the meat and vegetables until very well mixed.

1 (2-pound) top round roast

1 Cubanelle pepper, diced

1 large onion, diced

2 carrots, diced

28 ounces canned crushed tomatoes

2 cloves garlic

1 tablespoon oregano

½ teaspoon cumin

½ cup sliced green olives stuffed with pimento

Per Serving

Calories	Fat	Sodium	Carbohydrates	Fiber	Protein
260	11g	460mg	13g	3g	27g

Winter Borscht

1. In a nonstick skillet, sauté the beef for 1 minute. Drain off any excess fat.

2. Place the beef and the remaining ingredients in a 4-quart slow cooker. Cook on low for 8 hours. Stir before serving.

Per Serving

Calories	Fat	Sodium	Carbohydrates	Fiber	Protein
120	4g	340mg	7g	2g	14g

¾ pound lean top round beef, cubed

3½ cups shredded "Roasted" Beets (Chapter 10)

1 onion, diced

1 carrot, grated

½ teaspoon salt

½ teaspoon sugar

3 tablespoons red wine vinegar

½ teaspoon freshly ground black pepper

½ tablespoon dill seed

1 clove garlic, minced

1 cup shredded green cabbage

2 cups Roasted Vegetable Stock (Chapter 4) or beef broth

2 cups water

Red Wine Pot Roast

1. Pour the wine and water into an oval 4-quart slow cooker. Add the potatoes, carrots, fennel, rutabagas, onions, and garlic. Stir.

2. Add the beef. Sprinkle with salt and pepper. Cook on low for 8 hours.

3. Remove and slice the beef. Use a slotted spoon to serve the vegetables. Discard the cooking liquid.

Per Serving

Calories	Fat	Sodium	Carbohydrates	Fiber	Protein
320	4g	350mg	45g	9g	30g

⅓ cup red wine

½ cup water

4 red skin potatoes, quartered

3 carrots, cut into thirds

2 bulbs fennel, quartered

2 rutabagas, quartered

1 onion, sliced

4 cloves garlic, sliced

1 (1½-pound) lean top round roast, excess fat removed

½ teaspoon salt

½ teaspoon freshly ground black pepper

Beef Rogan Josh

1. In a nonstick skillet, sauté the beef, onions, and garlic until just browned. Drain off any excess fat. Place in a 4-quart slow cooker.

2. Add the spices and crushed tomatoes. Cook on low for 8 hours. Stir in the yogurt prior to serving.

Per Serving

Calories	Fat	Sodium	Carbohydrates	Fiber	Protein
230	10g	250mg	18g	4g	20g

1 pound bottom round roast, cubed

1 onion, diced

4 cloves garlic, minced

2 tablespoons cumin

2 tablespoons coriander

1 tablespoon turmeric

2 teaspoons cardamom

2 teaspoons minced fresh ginger

2 teaspoons freshly ground black pepper

2 teaspoons chili powder

28 ounces canned crushed tomatoes

1 cup fat-free Greek yogurt

Beef Biryani

1. Place the beef, spices, garlic, and onions in a 4-quart slow cooker. Stir. Cook on low for 7–8 hours.

2. About 30 minutes before serving, stir in the yogurt, peas, and rice. Cook on low for 30 minutes. Stir before serving.

Per Serving

Calories	Fat	Sodium	Carbohydrates	Fiber	Protein
230	7g	190mg	20g	2g	21g

1 pound top round roast, cut into strips

1 tablespoon minced fresh ginger

½ teaspoon ground cloves

½ teaspoon cardamom

½ teaspoon coriander

½ teaspoon freshly ground black pepper

½ teaspoon cinnamon

½ teaspoon cumin

¼ teaspoon salt

2 cloves garlic, minced

1 onion, minced

1 cup fat-free Greek yogurt

1 cup frozen peas

1½ cups cooked basmati or brown rice

Greek-Style Meatballs and Artichokes

1. Preheat the oven to 350°F. Place the bread and milk in a shallow saucepan. Cook on low until the milk is absorbed, about 1 minute. Place in a large bowl and add the pork, garlic, egg, zest, and pepper.

2. Mix until all ingredients are evenly distributed. Roll into 1" balls. Line two baking sheets with parchment paper. Place the meatballs in a single layer on the baking sheets. Bake for 15 minutes, and then drain on paper towel–lined plates.

3. Add the meatballs to a 6- or 7-quart slow cooker. Add the remaining ingredients. Cook on low for 6–8 hours.

2 thin slices white sandwich bread

½ cup 1% milk

2¾ pounds lean ground pork

2 cloves garlic, minced

1 egg

½ teaspoon lemon zest

¼ teaspoon freshly ground black pepper

16 ounces frozen **artichoke** hearts, defrosted

3 tablespoons lemon juice

2 cups Chicken Stock (Chapter 4)

¾ cup frozen chopped spinach

⅓ cup sliced Greek olives

1 tablespoon minced fresh oregano

Per Serving

Calories	Fat	Sodium	Carbohydrates	Fiber	Protein
400	28g	340mg	9g	<1g	25g

Pot Roast with Root Vegetables

Pot Roast with Root Vegetables

1. Pour the water into an oval 6-quart slow cooker. Add the potatoes, carrots, parsnips, rutabagas, onions, celeriac, and garlic. Stir.

2. Add the beef. Sprinkle with salt, paprika, and pepper. Cook on low for 8 hours.

3. Remove and slice the beef. Use a slotted spoon to serve the vegetables. Discard the cooking liquid.

1 cup water

4 russet potatoes, quartered

4 carrots, cut into thirds

4 parsnips, quartered

3 rutabagas, quartered

2 onions, sliced

1 celeriac, cubed

7 cloves garlic, sliced

1 (4–pound) lean top round beef roast, excess fat removed

½ teaspoon salt

1 teaspoon paprika

½ teaspoon freshly ground black pepper

Per Serving

Calories	Fat	Sodium	Carbohydrates	Fiber	Protein
310	5g	230mg	36g	7g	36g

Greek Boneless Leg of Lamb

1. Slice off any visible fat from the lamb and discard. Place in a 4- or 6-quart slow cooker.

2. Add the remaining ingredients on top of the lamb. Cook on low for 8 hours.

3. Remove from the slow cooker. Discard cooking liquid. Remove any remaining visible fat from the lamb. Slice the lamb just prior to serving.

1 (4-pound) boneless leg of lamb

1 tablespoon crushed rosemary

1 teaspoon freshly ground black pepper

¼ teaspoon kosher salt

¼ cup lemon juice

¼ cup water

Per Serving

Calories	Fat	Sodium	Carbohydrates	Fiber	Protein
350	21g	150mg	1g	0g	38g

Moroccan Lamb Stew

Place the lamb, garlic, onions, lemon juice, olives, honey, salt, pepper, and turmeric in a 2-quart slow cooker. Top with the sprigs of thyme. Cook on low for 8 hours.

½ pound lean boneless lamb, cubed

2 cloves garlic, minced

½ onion, chopped

2 tablespoons lemon juice

¼ cup sliced green olives

2 teaspoons honey

¼ teaspoon salt

½ teaspoon freshly ground black pepper

¼ teaspoon turmeric

2 sprigs fresh thyme

Per Serving

Calories	Fat	Sodium	Carbohydrates	Fiber	Protein
280	11g	630mg	13g	2g	32g

Mexican Stuffed Peppers

Mexican Stuffed Peppers

SERVES 2

1. Place the peppers on a broiler-safe tray. Broil on high for 2–5 minutes; flip and broil for 2–5 minutes on the other side. Rub each pepper with paper towels to remove the skin. Cut off the tops and cut a slit vertically down the middle of the pepper. Remove the seeds and discard them.

2. Heat the oil in a nonstick pan. Sauté the onions, jalapeños, corn, garlic, and meat until the onions are translucent.

3. Pour the meat mixture into a medium bowl. Stir in ¾ cup tomatoes. Divide the mixture and fill the peppers. "Close" the peppers by bringing both sides together.

4. Pour the remaining tomatoes onto the bottom of an oval 4-quart slow cooker. Top with the peppers. Cover and cook on low for 5 hours. Drizzle the sauce over the peppers prior to serving.

2 large poblano peppers

1 teaspoon canola oil

1 onion, diced

2 jalapeños, minced

¼ cup corn kernels

4 cloves garlic, minced

1 cup ground lamb, chicken, or turkey

28 ounces canned crushed tomatoes

Per Serving

Calories	Fat	Sodium	Carbohydrates	Fiber	Protein
370	8g	590mg	52g	14g	32g

Roast Beef

1. In a small bowl, stir the pepper, fennel seeds, rosemary, salt, and oregano. Rub it into all sides of the meat. Refrigerate for 15 minutes.

2. Place the roast in a 2-quart slow cooker. Add the Caramelized Onions, water or stock, and garlic. Cook on low for 8 hours. Remove and slice. Serve topped with the onions. Discard any cooking juices.

½ teaspoon freshly ground black pepper

½ teaspoon fennel seed

½ teaspoon crushed rosemary

¼ teaspoon salt

½ teaspoon dried oregano

1 (¾-pound) bottom round roast, excess fat removed

¼ cup Caramelized Onions (Chapter 5)

¼ cup water or beef stock

1 clove garlic, sliced

Per Serving

Calories	Fat	Sodium	Carbohydrates	Fiber	Protein
340	20g	390mg	2g	<1g	36g

Tamale Pie

1. Sauté the onions, ground beef, jalapeño, and garlic until the ground beef is browned. Drain off any excess fat.

2. Pour the ground beef mixture into a 4-quart slow cooker. Add the tomatoes, beans, chipotles, and chili powder. Cook on low for 8 hours.

3. In a medium bowl, mix the milk, oil, baking powder, cornmeal, and salt. Drop in ¼-cup mounds in a single layer on top of the beef. Cover and cook on high for 20 minutes without lifting the lid. The dumplings will look fluffy and light when fully cooked.

1 large onion, minced

1 pound 94% lean ground beef

1 jalapeño, minced

2 cloves garlic, minced

15 ounces canned diced tomatoes

10 ounces canned diced tomatoes with green chiles

15 ounces canned dark red kidney beans, drained and rinsed

4 chipotle peppers in adobo, minced

½ teaspoon hot Mexican chili powder

⅔ cup 2% milk

2 tablespoons canola oil

2 teaspoons baking powder

½ cup cornmeal

½ teaspoon salt

Per Serving

Calories	Fat	Sodium	Carbohydrates	Fiber	Protein
460	15g	1,300mg	47g	11g	36g

10

VEGETARIAN AND PESCATARIAN ENTRÉES

Fresh Chile Grits

1. Heat the canola oil in a small skillet. Add the onions and garlic and sauté until softened.
2. Add the onions, garlic, Roasted Vegetable Stock, grits, jalapeños, and spices to a 4-quart slow cooker. Stir. Cook on low for 8 hours. Stir the cheese into the grits before serving.

Per Serving

Calories	Fat	Sodium	Carbohydrates	Fiber	Protein
120	2.5g	180mg	21g	<1g	3g

1 tablespoon canola oil

1 medium onion, diced

2 cloves garlic, minced

4¼ cups Roasted Vegetable Stock (Chapter 4)

1½ cups stone-ground grits

4 jalapeños, sliced

1 teaspoon thyme

½ teaspoon freshly ground black pepper

¼ teaspoon salt

¼ cup shredded reduced-fat sharp vegetarian Cheddar

Curried Lentils

1. Heat the butter or oil in a nonstick pan. Sauté the onion slices until they start to brown, about 8–10 minutes. Add the garlic, jalapeños, red pepper flakes, and cumin. Sauté for 2–3 minutes.

2. Add the onion mixture to a 4-quart slow cooker. Sort through the lentils and discard any rocks or foreign matter. Add the lentils to the slow cooker. Stir in the water, salt, and turmeric.

3. Cook on high for 2½ hours. Add the spinach. Stir and cook on high for an additional 15 minutes.

2 teaspoons butter or canola oil

1 large onion, thinly sliced

2 cloves garlic, minced

2 jalapeños, diced

½ teaspoon red pepper flakes

½ teaspoon cumin

1 pound yellow lentils

6 cups water

½ teaspoon salt

½ teaspoon turmeric

4 cups chopped fresh spinach

Per Serving

Calories	Fat	Sodium	Carbohydrates	Fiber	Protein
280	2g	210mg	49g	10g	21g

10: VEGETARIAN AND PESCATARIAN ENTRÉES   213

Wild Mushroom Risotto

1. Heat the oil in a nonstick pan. Sauté the shallot, garlic, and mushrooms until soft. Add ½ cup Roasted Vegetable Stock and cook until half of the stock has evaporated. Add the rice and cook until the liquid is fully absorbed.

2. Scrape the rice mixture into a 4-quart slow cooker. Add the water and remaining stock, and cook on low for 1 hour. Stir before serving and garnish with parsley.

1 teaspoon olive oil

1 shallot, minced

2 cloves garlic, minced

8 ounces sliced assorted wild mushrooms

2 cups Roasted Vegetable Stock (Chapter 4), divided use

2 cups Arborio rice

3 cups water

1 tablespoon minced fresh parsley

Per Serving

Calories	Fat	Sodium	Carbohydrates	Fiber	Protein
150	1g	95mg	33g	<1g	5g

Wild Mushroom Risotto

Portobello Barley

1. Heat the oil in a nonstick skillet. Sauté the shallots, garlic, and mushrooms until softened.

2. Place the mushroom mixture in a 4-quart slow cooker. Add the barley, water, salt, pepper, rosemary, and chervil. Stir. Cook on low for 8–9 hours or on high for 4 hours.

3. Turn off the slow cooker and stir in the Parmesan. Serve immediately.

1 teaspoon olive oil

2 shallots, minced

2 cloves garlic, minced

3 Portobello mushroom caps, sliced

1 cup pearl barley

3¼ cups water

¼ teaspoon salt

½ teaspoon freshly ground black pepper

1 teaspoon crushed rosemary

1 teaspoon chervil

¼ cup grated vegetarian Parmesan

Per Serving

Calories	Fat	Sodium	Carbohydrates	Fiber	Protein
130	1.5g	120mg	25g	5g	5g

Thai Coconut Curry

1. Slice the tofu into ½"-thick triangles. Place in a 4-quart slow cooker. Top with coconut, water, garlic, ginger, galangal, onions, sweet potato, broccoli, snow peas, tamari, soy sauce, and chili-garlic sauce. Stir to distribute all ingredients evenly. Cook on low for 5 hours.

2. Stir in the cilantro and coconut milk. Cook on low for an additional 20 minutes. Stir prior to serving.

Per Serving

Calories	Fat	Sodium	Carbohydrates	Fiber	Protein
140	8g	870mg	13g	3g	7g

12 ounces extra-firm tofu

¼ cup unsweetened shredded coconut

¼ cup water

4 cloves garlic, minced

1 tablespoon minced fresh ginger

1 tablespoon minced galangal root

½ cup chopped onion

1 cup peeled and diced sweet potato

1 cup broccoli florets

1 cup snow peas

3 tablespoons tamari

1 tablespoon dark soy sauce

1 tablespoon chili-garlic sauce

½ cup minced fresh cilantro

½ cup light coconut milk

Cauliflower Chowder

1. Place the cauliflower, Roasted Vegetable Stock, onions, garlic, pepper, and salt in a 4-quart slow cooker. Stir. Cook on low for 6 hours or until the cauliflower is fork tender.

2. Use an immersion blender to purée the cauliflower in the slow cooker until very smooth. Add the broccoli, carrots, and celery. Cook on low for 30 minutes or until the vegetables are fork tender.

2 pounds cauliflower florets

2 quarts Roasted Vegetable Stock (Chapter 4) or water

1 onion, chopped

3 cloves garlic, minced

1 teaspoon white pepper

¼ teaspoon salt

1½ cups broccoli florets

2 carrots, cut into coins

1 stalk celery, diced

Per Serving

Calories	Fat	Sodium	Carbohydrates	Fiber	Protein
90	1g	540mg	16g	6g	6g

Herb-Stuffed Tomatoes

1. Cut out the core of each tomato and discard. Scoop out the seeds, leaving the walls of the tomato intact.

2. In a small bowl, stir together the quinoa, celery, garlic, and spices. Divide evenly among the four tomatoes.

3. Place the filled tomatoes in a single layer in an oval 4-quart slow cooker. Pour the water into the bottom of the slow cooker. Cook on low for 4 hours.

4 large tomatoes

1 cup cooked quinoa

1 stalk celery, minced

1 tablespoon minced fresh garlic

2 tablespoons minced fresh oregano

2 tablespoons minced fresh Italian parsley

1 teaspoon dried chervil

1 teaspoon fennel seed

¾ cup water

Per Serving

Calories	Fat	Sodium	Carbohydrates	Fiber	Protein
210	3.5g	30mg	39g	5g	8g

Eggplant Caponata

Eggplant Caponata

1. Pierce the eggplants with a fork. Cook on high in a 4- or 6-quart slow cooker for 2 hours.

2. Allow to cool. Peel off the skin. Slice each in half and remove the seeds. Discard the skin and seeds.

3. Place the pulp in a food processor and pulse until smooth. Set aside.

4. Heat the oil in a nonstick skillet. Sauté the onions, garlic, and celery until the onions are soft. Add the eggplant and tomatoes. Sauté 3 minutes.

5. Pour the eggplant mixture into the slow cooker and add the capers, pine nuts, red pepper flakes, and vinegar. Stir. Cook on low 30 minutes. Stir prior to serving and garnish with basil leaves.

2 (1-pound) eggplants

1 teaspoon olive oil

1 red onion, diced

4 cloves garlic, minced

1 stalk celery, diced

2 tomatoes, diced

2 tablespoons nonpareil capers

2 tablespoons toasted pine nuts

1 teaspoon red pepper flakes

¼ cup red wine vinegar

1 tablespoon minced fresh basil

Per Serving

Calories	Fat	Sodium	Carbohydrates	Fiber	Protein
70	2.5g	75mg	11g	5g	2g

Gumbo z'Herbs

1. Tear the mustard greens, turnip greens, beet greens, and spinach into bite-sized pieces. Discard the ribs. Thoroughly clean the greens of any grit.

2. Heat the oil in a large pot. Add the onions, garlic, celery, and peppers, and sauté 3 minutes. Add all of the greens and stir until the greens start to wilt. Add to a 4- or 6-quart slow cooker.

3. Add the remaining ingredients to the slow cooker. Stir. Cook on low for 6 hours. Stir prior to serving.

Per Serving

Calories	Fat	Sodium	Carbohydrates	Fiber	Protein
140	2.5g	810mg	27g	11g	9g

1 bunch mustard greens

1 bunch turnip greens

1 bunch beet greens

1 bunch spinach

1 teaspoon canola oil

2 onions, diced

6 cloves garlic, minced

2 stalks celery (including greens), diced

2 bell peppers, chopped

1 bunch dandelion greens, chopped

1 bunch watercress, chopped

1 bunch carrot tops, chopped

1½ cups shredded cabbage

1½ cups chopped butter lettuce

2 large turnips, diced

1 cup diced green onions

3½ quarts Roasted Vegetable Stock (Chapter 4) or water

1 tablespoon hickory liquid smoke

1 tablespoon minced fresh thyme

1 teaspoon red pepper flakes

½ teaspoon freshly ground black pepper

½ teaspoon ground cloves

½ teaspoon allspice

¼ teaspoon salt

Sweet and Sour Tofu

1. Spray a nonstick skillet with cooking spray. Sauté the tofu until it is lightly browned on all sides. Add to a 4-quart slow cooker.

2. In a small bowl, whisk together the vinegar, water, sesame seeds, brown sugar, tamari, pineapple juice, and ginger until the sugar fully dissolves. Pour over the tofu.

3. Add the remaining ingredients. Cook on low for 4 hours. Remove the lid and cook on low for 30 minutes.

12 ounces extra-firm tofu, cubed

¼ cup rice vinegar

3 tablespoons water

1 tablespoon sesame seeds

1 tablespoon brown sugar

1 tablespoon tamari

1 tablespoon pineapple juice

1 teaspoon ground ginger

¾ cup pineapple chunks

1 cup snow peas

½ cup sliced onion

Per Serving

Calories	Fat	Sodium	Carbohydrates	Fiber	Protein
80	2g	210mg	10g	1g	5g

Chickpea Curry

1. Place the chickpeas in a 4-quart slow cooker. Fill the rest of the insert with water. Allow the chickpeas to soak overnight. Drain and return to the slow cooker.

2. Heat the oil in a nonstick pan. Sauté the onions, garlic, and ginger until the onions are soft and translucent. Add to the slow cooker.

3. Add the remaining ingredients. Stir. Cook on low for 8–10 hours. Stir before serving.

1 cup dried chickpeas

Water, as needed

1 teaspoon olive oil

1 onion, diced

3 cloves garlic, minced

1 tablespoon minced fresh ginger

1 large tomato, diced

2 tablespoons tomato paste

1 tablespoon cumin

1 teaspoon turmeric

1 teaspoon coriander

1 teaspoon asafetida powder

1 teaspoon cayenne

¼ teaspoon cinnamon

Per Serving

Calories	Fat	Sodium	Carbohydrates	Fiber	Protein
110	2g	40mg	19g	4g	6g

"Roasted" Beets

1. Place the beets in the bottom of a 4-quart slow cooker. Pour the lemon juice and vinegar over the top. Cook on low for 2 hours or until they are easily pierced with a fork.

2. Remove from the slow cooker. Allow to cool slightly. Wrap a beet in a paper towel and rub it to remove the skin. Repeat for the remaining beets.

2 pounds whole beets, stems and leaves removed

2 tablespoons lemon juice

¼ cup balsamic vinegar

Per Serving

Calories	Fat	Sodium	Carbohydrates	Fiber	Protein
60	0g	90mg	14g	3g	2g

White Bean Cassoulet

1. The night before making the soup, place the beans in a 4-quart slow cooker. Fill with water to 1" below the top of the insert. Soak overnight.

2. Drain the beans and return them to the slow cooker.

3. Pour the boiling water over the dried mushrooms in a heat-proof bowl and soak for 15 minutes. Slice only the white and light green parts of the leeks into ¼" rounds. Cut the rounds in half.

4. Heat the oil in a nonstick skillet. Add the parsnips, carrots, celery, and leeks. Sauté for 1 minute, just until the color of the vegetables brightens. Add to the slow cooker along with the spices.

5. Add the mushrooms, their soaking liquid, and the Roasted Vegetable Stock. Stir. Cook on low for 8–10 hours.

1 pound dried cannellini beans

2 cups boiling water

1 ounce dried porcini mushrooms

2 leeks, sliced

1 teaspoon canola oil

2 parsnips, diced

2 carrots, diced

2 stalks celery, diced

½ teaspoon fennel seed

1 teaspoon crushed rosemary

1 teaspoon chervil

⅛ teaspoon ground cloves

¼ teaspoon salt

¼ teaspoon freshly ground black pepper

2 cups Roasted Vegetable Stock (Chapter 4)

Per Serving

Calories	Fat	Sodium	Carbohydrates	Fiber	Protein
220	1.5g	170mg	39g	10g	15g

Stuffed Peppers

1. Cut the top off of each pepper to form a cap. Remove the seeds from the cap. Remove the seeds and most of the ribs inside the pepper. Place the peppers open-side up in an oval 4- or 6-quart slow cooker.

2. In a medium bowl, mix the spices, tomatoes, rice, broccoli, and onions. Spoon the mixture into each pepper until they are filled to the top. Replace the cap. Pour the water into the bottom of the slow cooker insert.

3. Cook on low for 6 hours.

Per Serving

Calories	Fat	Sodium	Carbohydrates	Fiber	Protein
140	0.5g	580mg	30g	5g	4g

4 large bell peppers

½ teaspoon ground chipotle

¼ teaspoon hot Mexican chili powder

¼ teaspoon freshly ground black pepper

⅛ teaspoon salt

15 ounces canned fire-roasted diced tomatoes with garlic

1 cup cooked long-grain rice

1½ cups broccoli florets

¼ cup diced onion

½ cup water

Miso Soup with Tofu and Wakame

1. Pour the water into a 4-quart slow cooker. Whisk in the miso paste until it is fully dissolved. Add the tofu. Cook on low for 8 hours.

2. Add the seaweed and green onions. Cook on high for 15 minutes. Stir before serving.

2 quarts water

3–4 tablespoons white miso paste

12 ounces extra-firm tofu, diced

1 cup broken, dried wakame seaweed

1 bunch green onions, diced

Per Serving

Calories	Fat	Sodium	Carbohydrates	Fiber	Protein
60	1g	460mg	6g	2g	7g

Miso Soup with Tofu and Wakame

Palak Tofu

1. Cut the tofu into ½" cubes. Set aside.

2. Heat the oil in a nonstick skillet. Sauté the cumin seeds for 1 minute, then add the garlic and jalapeños. Sauté until fragrant, then add the tofu and potatoes. Sauté for 3 minutes. Add the ginger, garam masala, frozen spinach, and cilantro. Sauté 1 minute.

3. Pour the mixture into a 4-quart slow cooker and cook on low for 4 hours.

14 ounces extra-firm tofu

1 tablespoon canola oil

1 teaspoon cumin seeds

2 cloves garlic, minced

2 jalapeños, minced

¾ pound red skin potatoes, diced

½ teaspoon ground ginger

¾ teaspoon garam masala

1 pound frozen cut-leaf spinach

¼ cup chopped fresh cilantro

Per Serving

Calories	Fat	Sodium	Carbohydrates	Fiber	Protein
190	7g	150mg	22g	5g	14g

Stuffed Eggplant

1. Preheat oven to 375°F. Slice the eggplant lengthwise into 2 equal halves. Use an ice cream scoop to take out the seeds. Place eggplant on a baking sheet, skin-side down. Bake for 8 minutes, then allow to cool slightly.

2. Heat the oil in a small skillet. Sauté the onions and garlic until softened.

3. In a medium bowl, stir the onions, garlic, rice, parsley, corn, and mushrooms. Divide evenly among the wells in the eggplant.

4. Pour the tomatoes onto the bottom of an oval 4- or 6-quart slow cooker. Place the eggplant halves side by side. Cook on low for 3 hours.

5. Remove the eggplants and plate.

1 (1-pound) eggplant

½ teaspoon olive oil

2 tablespoons minced red onion

1 clove garlic, minced

⅓ cup cooked rice

1 tablespoon minced fresh parsley

¼ cup corn kernels

¼ cup diced crimini mushrooms

15 ounces canned diced tomatoes with onions and garlic

Per Serving

Calories	Fat	Sodium	Carbohydrates	Fiber	Protein
190	3.5g	1,040mg	41g	10g	8g

Korean-Style Hot Pot

1. Remove the leaves of the baby bok choy. Wash thoroughly. Place them whole in a 4-quart slow cooker. Add the water, crimini mushrooms, tofu, garlic, sesame oil, and red pepper flakes. Stir.

2. Cook on low for 8 hours. Add the enoki mushrooms and stir. Cook an additional ½ hour before serving.

3 bunches baby bok choy

8 cups water

8 ounces sliced crimini mushrooms

12 ounces extra-firm tofu, cubed

3 cloves garlic, thinly sliced

¼ teaspoon sesame oil

1 tablespoon red pepper flakes

7 ounces enoki mushrooms

Per Serving

Calories	Fat	Sodium	Carbohydrates	Fiber	Protein
80	2g	230mg	11g	4g	9g

Green Chile and Hominy Stew

1. Heat the oil in a nonstick pan. Sauté the Cubanelle peppers, canned green peppers, jalapeños, onions, and garlic until fragrant.

2. Add the mixture to a 4-quart slow cooker. Add the water, hominy, salt, pepper, and ground jalapeño. Stir. Cook on low for 7 hours.

3. Add the zucchini and cook on high for 1 hour. Stir prior to serving.

1 teaspoon canola oil

2 Cubanelle peppers, diced

4 ounces canned diced green peppers

2 jalapeños, diced

1 onion, diced

4 cloves garlic, minced

3¾ cups water

24 ounces canned hominy

¼ teaspoon salt

½ teaspoon freshly ground black pepper

½ teaspoon ground jalapeño

3 zucchini, diced

Per Serving

Calories	Fat	Sodium	Carbohydrates	Fiber	Protein
130	2g	420mg	25g	5g	4g

Salmon with Lemon, Capers, and Rosemary

Salmon with Lemon, Capers, and Rosemary

1. Place the salmon on the bottom of a 2-quart slow cooker. Pour the water and lemon juice over the fish. Arrange the lemon slices in a single layer on top of the fish. Sprinkle with capers and rosemary.

2. Cook on low for 2 hours. Discard lemon slices prior to serving. Serve with vegetables and fresh lemon slices.

8 ounces salmon

⅓ cup water

2 tablespoons lemon juice

3 thin slices fresh lemon

1 tablespoon nonpareil capers

½ teaspoon minced fresh rosemary

Per Serving

Calories	Fat	Sodium	Carbohydrates	Fiber	Protein
170	7g	180mg	2g	0g	23g

Hawaiian-Style Mahi-Mahi

1. Place the fillets in a 6-quart slow cooker. Top with the remaining ingredients. Cook on low 5 hours or until the fish is fully cooked.

2. Remove the fillets and discard the cooking liquid.

6 (4-ounce) mahi-mahi fillets

12 ounces pineapple juice

3 tablespoons grated fresh ginger

¼ cup lime juice

3 tablespoons ponzu sauce

Per Serving

Calories	Fat	Sodium	Carbohydrates	Fiber	Protein
140	1g	100mg	10g	0g	21g

Low Country Boil

1. Place the corn, potatoes, seasoning, mustard seeds, onions, and bay leaf in a 6- or 7-quart slow cooker. Fill the insert with water to about 2½" below the top.

2. Cook on high for 2½ hours or until the corn and potatoes are tender. Add the shrimp and continue to cook on high for 20 minutes or until thoroughly cooked.

Per Serving

Calories	Fat	Sodium	Carbohydrates	Fiber	Protein
240	3g	280mg	30g	3g	21g

4 ears corn, halved

1½ pounds baby red skin potatoes

¼ cup Chesapeake Bay seasoning or shrimp boil seasoning

1 tablespoon yellow mustard seeds

2 large onions, thinly sliced

1 bay leaf

Water, as needed

1½ pounds medium shrimp

Ginger-Lime Salmon

1. Place the salmon skin-side down in an oval 6- or 7-quart slow cooker. Pour the ginger and lime juice over the fish. Arrange the lime slices and then the onions in single layers over the fish.

2. Cook on low for 3–4 hours or until the fish is fully cooked and flaky. Remove the skin before serving.

1 (3-pound) salmon fillet, bones removed

¼ cup minced fresh ginger

¼ cup lime juice

1 lime, thinly sliced

1 onion, thinly sliced

Per Serving

Calories	Fat	Sodium	Carbohydrates	Fiber	Protein
170	7g	50mg	2g	0g	23g

Catfish Smothered in Onions

1. Heat the oil in a nonstick pan. Sauté the onions, garlic, and jalapeño until softened.

2. Place the catfish in a 2-quart slow cooker. Top with remaining ingredients. Cook on low for 2½ hours or until the fish is fully cooked through.

½ teaspoon canola oil

2 onions, sliced

2 cloves garlic, minced

1 jalapeño, diced

2 catfish fillets

1 small tomato, diced

½ teaspoon hot sauce

½ teaspoon Creole seasoning

Per Serving

Calories	Fat	Sodium	Carbohydrates	Fiber	Protein
300	13g	270mg	17g	4g	27g

11

SWEETS AND DESSERTS

Light and Creamy Hot Fudge Sauce

1. Place all ingredients in a 1½- or 2-quart slow cooker. Cook on low, stirring occasionally, for 2 hours. The sauce will thicken as it cools.

2. Refrigerate leftovers. Reheat in the slow cooker for 1 hour on high or on the stovetop until warmed through, about 10 minutes.

12 ounces fat-free evaporated milk

10 ounces semisweet or bittersweet chocolate chips

1 teaspoon vanilla

½ teaspoon butter

⅛ teaspoon salt

Per Serving

Calories	Fat	Sodium	Carbohydrates	Fiber	Protein
60	3g	25mg	7g	<1g	1g

Green Tea Tapioca Pudding

1. Pour the evaporated milk, tapioca, matcha, and sugar into a 4-quart slow cooker. Whisk until the sugar dissolves. Cook on low for 1½ hours.

2. Stir in the egg. Cook on low for an additional ½ hour. Serve warm.

2 cups fat-free evaporated milk

¼ cup small pearl tapioca

1 teaspoon matcha or green tea powder

½ cup sugar

1 egg

Per Serving

Calories	Fat	Sodium	Carbohydrates	Fiber	Protein
170	1g	110mg	32g	0g	8g

Challah Bread Pudding

1. Spray a 4-quart slow cooker with cooking spray. Add the bread cubes and dried fruit. Stir.
2. In a medium bowl, whisk the evaporated milk, eggs, brown sugar, vanilla, cinnamon, ginger, and nutmeg. Pour over the bread cubes and dried fruit.
3. Cook on low for 5 hours.

4 cups cubed challah

⅓ cup dried tart cherries or cranberries

2⅓ cups fat-free evaporated milk

2 eggs

⅓ cup dark brown sugar

1 teaspoon vanilla extract

1 teaspoon cinnamon

½ teaspoon ground ginger

¼ teaspoon nutmeg

Per Serving

Calories	Fat	Sodium	Carbohydrates	Fiber	Protein
140	2g	150mg	24g	<1g	7g

Slow-Cooked Pineapple

Place all ingredients in a 4-quart oval slow cooker. Cook on low for 4 hours or until fork tender. Remove the vanilla bean before serving.

1 whole pineapple, peeled

1 vanilla bean, split

3 tablespoons water or rum

Per Serving

Calories	Fat	Sodium	Carbohydrates	Fiber	Protein
35	0g	0mg	8g	<1g	0g

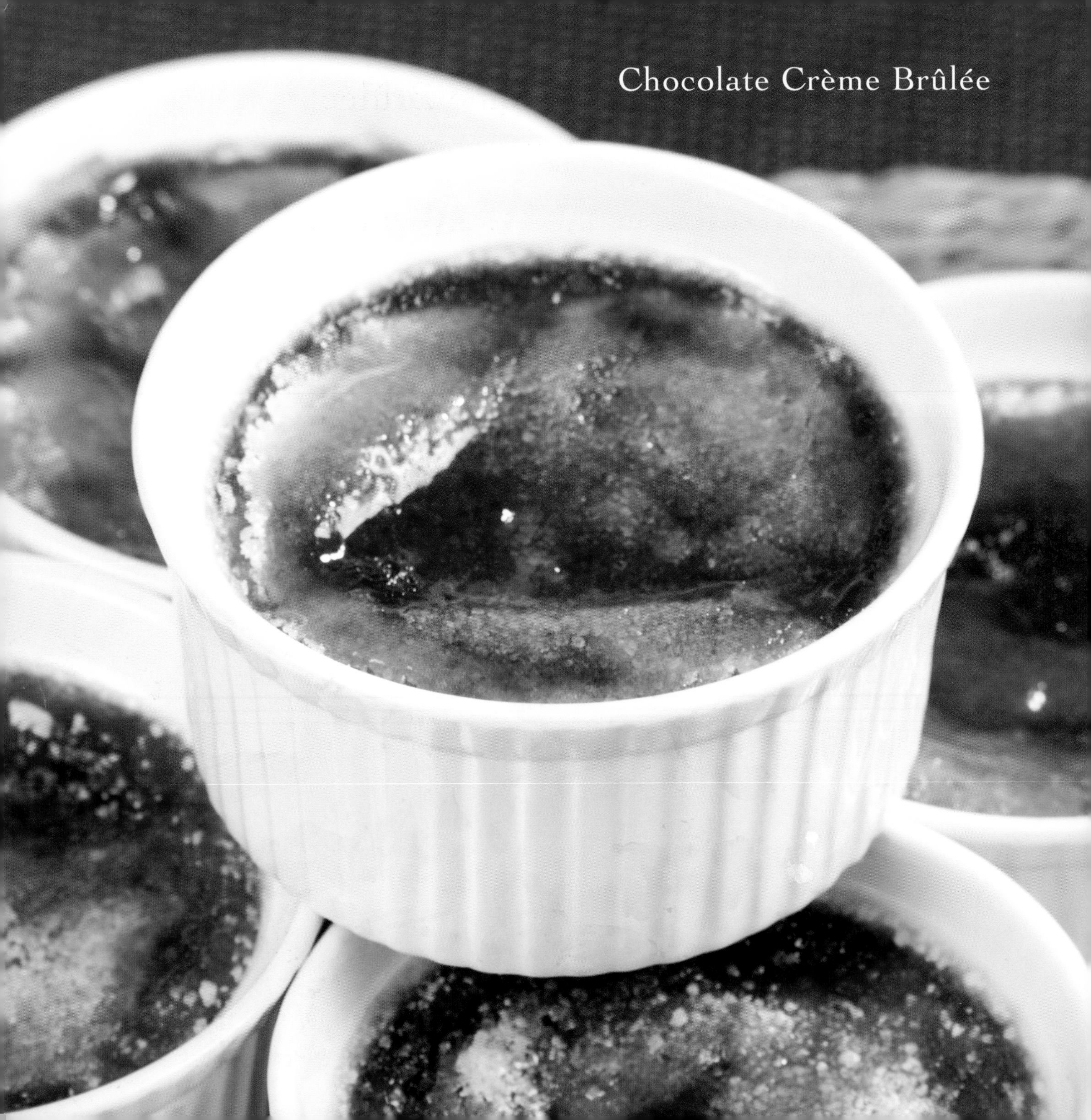
Chocolate Crème Brûlée

Chocolate Crème Brûlée

1. In a small bowl, whisk the evaporated milk, cocoa, vanilla, egg yolks, and sugar until the sugar dissolves. Pour the mixture into a small pan and bring it to a boil. Remove the pan from the heat and allow the mixture to cool. Divide it among four 5- or 6-ounce broiler-safe ramekins.

2. Pour 1" of water into the bottom of an oval 6-quart slow cooker. Place the ramekins in the water. Cook on high for 3 hours or until the custard is set.

3. Sprinkle each crème brûlée with ½ tablespoon brown sugar. Place them under the broiler and broil until the sugar caramelizes.

2 cups fat-free evaporated milk

2½ tablespoons cocoa

½ teaspoon vanilla extract

4 egg yolks

½ cup sugar

2 tablespoons brown sugar

Per Serving

Calories	Fat	Sodium	Carbohydrates	Fiber	Protein
290	5g	160mg	49g	1g	13g

Cheesecake

1. In a small bowl, mix together the graham cracker crumbs and butter. Press into the bottom and sides of a 6" spring-form pan.

2. In a large bowl, mix the sour cream, cream cheese, sugar, egg, vanilla, flour, lemon juice, and zest until completely smooth. Pour into the springform pan.

3. Pour 1" of water into the bottom of a 6-quart slow cooker. Place a trivet in the bottom of the slow cooker. Place the pan onto the trivet.

4. Cook on low for 2 hours. Turn off the slow cooker and let the cheesecake steam for 1 hour and 15 minutes with the lid on. Remove the cheesecake from the slow cooker. Refrigerate 6 hours or overnight before serving.

¾ cup reduced-fat chocolate or cinnamon graham cracker crumbs

1½ tablespoons butter, melted

8 ounces reduced-fat sour cream, at room temperature

8 ounces reduced-fat cream cheese, at room temperature

⅔ cup sugar

1 egg, at room temperature

1 tablespoon vanilla paste or vanilla extract

1½ tablespoons flour

1 tablespoon lemon juice

1 tablespoon lemon zest

Per Serving

Calories	Fat	Sodium	Carbohydrates	Fiber	Protein
240	12g	150mg	28g	0g	5g

Pear and Cranberry Crumble

1. Spray a 2-quart slow cooker with nonstick spray. Add the pears, cranberries, and brown sugar. Stir. Cook on high for 3 hours.

2. In a small bowl, whisk the butter, oats, flour, cinnamon, nutmeg, and sugar. Sprinkle over the fruit and cook on high for 30 minutes. Remove the lid and cook, uncovered, on high for an additional 10 minutes.

Per Serving

Calories	Fat	Sodium	Carbohydrates	Fiber	Protein
150	4.5g	0mg	26g	4g	2g

3 Bosc pears, thinly sliced

¾ cup fresh cranberries

2 tablespoons light brown sugar

2 tablespoons melted unsalted butter

½ cup old-fashioned rolled oats

⅛ cup flour

½ teaspoon cinnamon

⅛ teaspoon nutmeg

½ tablespoon sugar

Orange-Scented Custard

Place all ingredients in a large bowl. Whisk until smooth. Pour into a 4-quart slow cooker. Cook on low for 8 hours, or until the center looks set and does not jiggle.

1 tablespoon orange blossom water, or ½ teaspoon orange extract

2 cups fat-free evaporated milk

5 eggs

⅓ cup sugar

Per Serving

Calories	Fat	Sodium	Carbohydrates	Fiber	Protein
100	2.5g	95mg	13g	0g	7g

Chai Pudding

1. Steep the tea bags in the evaporated milk for 20 minutes. Discard the bags. Whisk in the brown sugar, spices, and tapioca.

2. Pour the mixture into a 2- or 4-quart slow cooker and cook on low for 1½ hours. Stir in the egg and continue to cook for 30 minutes.

2 chai tea bags

2 cups fat-free evaporated milk

⅓ cup brown sugar

½ teaspoon cinnamon

½ teaspoon ground star anise

½ teaspoon mace

½ teaspoon cardamom

¼ cup small pearl tapioca

1 egg

Per Serving

Calories	Fat	Sodium	Carbohydrates	Fiber	Protein
150	1g	115mg	28g	0g	8g

Brown Bread

1. Grease the insides of the empty cans with cooking spray. Place a layer of bamboo skewers on the bottom of an oval 6-quart slow cooker. Place the cans upright on the skewers.

2. In a medium bowl, whisk together the flours, cornmeal, sugar, baking powder, baking soda, cinnamon, cranberries, and ginger. Set the mixture aside. In another bowl, stir together the buttermilk and molasses. Pour into the dry mixture and stir until combined.

3. Evenly divide the dough among the three cans and cover the top of each can with foil; stand the cans inside the slow cooker. Add water to the cooker until it is halfway up the sides of the cans. Cook on low for 4–5 hours or until a toothpick inserted into the bread comes out clean.

4. Carefully remove the cans and allow them to cool for 5 minutes. Then gently tap the cans and remove the bread. Allow the bread to cool on a wire rack. Slice each loaf into 20 slices.

3 empty 16-ounce cans, cleaned and with labels removed, one end still intact

Nonstick cooking spray, as needed

Bamboo skewers, to fit slow cooker

½ cup rye flour

½ cup all-purpose flour

½ cup cornmeal

1 tablespoon sugar

½ teaspoon baking powder

½ teaspoon baking soda

½ teaspoon cinnamon

½ cup sweetened dried cranberries

½ teaspoon ground ginger

1 cup fat-free buttermilk

⅓ cup molasses

Water, as needed

Per Serving

Calories	Fat	Sodium	Carbohydrates	Fiber	Protein
70	0.5g	55mg	15g	<1g	1g

Vanilla Poached
Pears

Vanilla Poached Pears

Stand the pears up in a 4-quart oval slow cooker. Add the remaining ingredients. Cook on low for 2 hours or until the pears are tender. Discard all cooking liquid prior to serving.

4 Bosc pears, peeled
1 vanilla bean, split
2 tablespoons vanilla extract
2 cups water

Per Serving

Calories	Fat	Sodium	Carbohydrates	Fiber	Protein
100	0g	0mg	22g	4g	1g

Caramel Popcorn

1. Place the brown sugar and butter in a 4-quart slow cooker. Cook on high for 1 hour, stirring occasionally, until caramel forms.

2. Drizzle over popcorn and toss. Serve immediately.

1½ cups light brown sugar
2 tablespoons butter, cubed
8 quarts air-popped popcorn

Per Serving

Calories	Fat	Sodium	Carbohydrates	Fiber	Protein
200	3g	25mg	43g	3g	3g

"Baked" Apples

1. Place the apples in a single layer on the bottom of a 4- or 6-quart slow cooker. Add the water, cinnamon stick, ginger, and vanilla bean. Cook on low for 6–8 hours or until the apples are tender and easily pierced with a fork.

2. Use a slotted spoon to remove the apples from the insert. Discard the cinnamon stick, ginger, vanilla bean, and water. Serve hot.

6 baking apples

½ cup water

1 cinnamon stick

1" knob peeled fresh ginger

1 vanilla bean

Per Serving

Calories	Fat	Sodium	Carbohydrates	Fiber	Protein
80	0g	0mg	20g	4g	0g

Poached Figs

1. Put all ingredients into a 2-quart slow cooker. Cook on low for 5 hours or until the figs are cooked through and starting to split.

2. Remove the figs from the poaching liquid and serve.

8 ounces fresh figs

1 cup water

1 vanilla bean, split

1 tablespoon sugar

Per Serving

Calories	Fat	Sodium	Carbohydrates	Fiber	Protein
60	0g	0mg	14g	2g	0g

Appendix: Metric Conversion Chart

VOLUME CONVERSIONS

U.S. Volume Measure	Metric Equivalent
⅛ teaspoon	0.5 milliliter
¼ teaspoon	1 milliliter
½ teaspoon	2 milliliters
1 teaspoon	5 milliliters
½ tablespoon	7 milliliters
1 tablespoon (3 teaspoons)	15 milliliters
2 tablespoons (1 fluid ounce)	30 milliliters
¼ cup (4 tablespoons)	60 milliliters
⅓ cup	90 milliliters
½ cup (4 fluid ounces)	125 milliliters
⅔ cup	160 milliliters
¾ cup (6 fluid ounces)	180 milliliters
1 cup (16 tablespoons)	250 milliliters
1 pint (2 cups)	500 milliliters
1 quart (4 cups)	1 liter (about)

WEIGHT CONVERSIONS

U.S. Weight Measure	Metric Equivalent
½ ounce	15 grams
1 ounce	30 grams
2 ounces	60 grams
3 ounces	85 grams
¼ pound (4 ounces)	115 grams
½ pound (8 ounces)	225 grams
¾ pound (12 ounces)	340 grams
1 pound (16 ounces)	454 grams

OVEN TEMPERATURE CONVERSIONS

Degrees Fahrenheit	Degrees Celsius
200 degrees F	95 degrees C
250 degrees F	120 degrees C
275 degrees F	135 degrees C
300 degrees F	150 degrees C
325 degrees F	160 degrees C
350 degrees F	180 degrees C
375 degrees F	190 degrees C
400 degrees F	205 degrees C
425 degrees F	220 degrees C
450 degrees F	230 degrees C

BAKING PAN SIZES

American	Metric
8 x 1½ inch round baking pan	20 x 4 cm cake tin
9 x 1½ inch round baking pan	23 x 3.5 cm cake tin
11 x 7 x 1½ inch baking pan	28 x 18 x 4 cm baking tin
13 x 9 x 2 inch baking pan	30 x 20 x 5 cm baking tin
2 quart rectangular baking dish	30 x 20 x 3 cm baking tin
15 x 10 x 2 inch baking pan	30 x 25 x 2 cm baking tin (Swiss roll tin)
9 inch pie plate	22 x 4 or 23 x 4 cm pie plate
7 or 8 inch springform pan	18 or 20 cm springform or loose bottom cake tin
9 x 5 x 3 inch loaf pan	23 x 13 x 7 cm or 2 lb narrow loaf or pate tin
1½ quart casserole	1.5 liter casserole
2 quart casserole	2 liter casserole

Index